Elihu

YALE

Merchant, Collector & Patron

Diana Scarisbrick and
Benjamin Zucker

Elihu YALE

Merchant, Collector & Patron

Thames & Hudson

First published in 2014 in hardcover
in the United States of America by
Thames & Hudson Inc., 500 Fifth Avenue,
New York, New York 10110

thamesandhudsonusa.com

Library of Congress Catalog Card Number
2013948276

ISBN 978-0-500-51726-0

Printed and bound in China by
C & C Offset Printing Co. Ltd

FRONTISPIECE

1. Portrait of Elihu Yale by Enoch Seeman
the Younger, 1717 – the year in which he was
elected to the Royal Society and to the Society
for the Propagation of the Gospel in Foreign
Parts. The artist has given us a glimpse of
shipping in the background, to evoke Yale's
connection with the East India Company. The
portrait was given to Yale University by Elihu's
great-grandson, Dudley Long North.

CONTENTS

PART I
MERCHANT, GENTLEMAN, PHILANTHROPIST

PART II
DEALER & COLLECTOR IN LONDON

CONCLUSION

PART I

———

MERCHANT, GENTLEMAN, PHILANTHROPIST

1

BOSTON TO FORT
ST GEORGE

No other nation made such a positive attempt to attract private traders
of all nations and religions nor showed as much honour to the Hindus as
the East India Company.

—Edgar Samuel[1]

There can be few educational institutions named after a man with
the force of character, powers of leadership, business acumen, and
variety of intellectual and spiritual interests of Elihu Yale (1649–
1721) [1]. The story of his life, which reveals the tenacity he showed
in overcoming professional difficulties and in his determination to
educate his mind despite his lack of academic training, establishes
him as someone of whom Yale University and its alumni can feel
proud. In addition, his career, which spans Puritan New England,
Mughal India, and the London of the English Enlightenment,
throws light on the religious, political, social, commercial, scientific, and cultural circumstances of the world of the later Stuarts
and early Hanoverians.

His father, David Yale (1614–90), was a 'stout-hearted and
God-fearing' Welsh merchant owning property at Plas Grono near
Wrexham in North Wales [69], who in 1637 emigrated to the New
World, risking the hard three-thousand-mile journey in the hope of
finding better business opportunities and greater religious freedom
than in the England of Charles I. When life in the Puritan community
of New Haven proved a disappointment David and his wife Ursula
moved to Boston, where their son was born; he was named after the
Biblical figure Elihu, who discussed the power and justice of God with
Job (Book of Job, chapters 32–37). The infant's future career was to
show how much he had inherited from his father: his Welsh nation-
alism, Protestant faith, trading background, and independent spirit.

This last was manifested when David, whose political and religious ideas conflicted with those of the New England authorities, instead of conforming removed his young family back to England in 1652 and set himself up in business in London, under the Commonwealth. Soon disillusioned with Republicanism, headopted Tory views, upholding the monarchy and the established religion.[2] The young Elihu went to the Merchant Taylors' School, and grew up in the momentous times when the government changed from the Commonwealth of Oliver Cromwell to the Restoration of Charles II, and the City was threatened by the Plague of 1665, followed by the Great Fire [124], which destroyed thirteen thousand houses and eighty-nine churches. After working in his father's counting house, Elihu Yale was accepted as a clerk by the East India Company in 1671, and a year later was appointed as writer (a junior clerical officer), at an annual salary of £10, to join the small English community at Fort St George in Madras [19] (renamed Chennai in the 20th century) – either to make his fortune or to die of a fever.

The East India Company, founded in England to trade with India and the Far East, was incorporated by royal charter in 1600. By 1610–11 relations were established with the court of the Great Mogul, and small settlements or factories had been built on the coast of the Bay of Bengal. After many disputes with Dutch, French and Portuguese rivals, the Company began the extraordinary ascent that culminated two hundred years later in the British domination of the Indian subcontinent. This development could hardly have been predicted in the middle years of the 17th century, when the Company's holdings consisted of no more than, in the words of T. B. Macaulay (who served on the Supreme Council of India in the 1830s), 'a few square miles of territory for which rent was paid to the native governments'.

HET HUIS VAN DEN OOST INDISCHE COMPAGNIE IN LON DEN

2. The early 17th-century façade of the Old East India House in Leadenhall Street, London, was surmounted by the figure of a seaman between dolphins, above a painting of the East India Company's ships at sea.

Its troops were scarcely numerous enough to man the batteries of three or four ill-constructed forts, which had been erected for the protection of the warehouses. The natives, who composed a considerable part of these little garrisons, had not yet been trained in the discipline of Europe and were armed, some with swords and shields, some with bows and arrows. The business of the servant of the company was to take stock, to make advances to the weavers, to ship cargoes, and above all to keep an eye on private traders who dared to infringe the monopoly.[3]

The headquarters building in the City of London, which survived the fire of 1666, was an 'edifice of timber and plaster, rich with the quaint carving and latticework of the Elizabethan age. Above the windows was a painting representing a fleet of merchantmen tossing on the waves. The whole was surmounted by a colossal wooden seaman, who from between two dolphins looked down on [the] crowds of Leadenhall Street' [2].[4] From there a succession of all-powerful directors, culminating in the ruthless Sir Josiah Child [15], exercised, notwithstanding the distance, a despotic control over every detail of life in the settlements, and made enormous profits (see p. 49). From the beginning they were suspicious of fraud and theft at every level, preferring to employ an honest man of average ability to 'a man of parts that is a knave'. This recognition of human weakness was demonstrated in 1603 when the porters engaged in unloading a cargo of valuable pepper were issued with suits of canvas and hose with no pockets.[5]

As the directors were equally determined to uphold the established religion, the captains of the Company ships and the governors of settlements were required to hold daily prayers. Services were held in thanksgiving for the safe arrival of a ship, and in return for alms the poor were asked to pray 'for the good and prosperitie of their voyadges'.[6] A hospital – a hostel – was founded at Poplar, east of the City, for 'maimed men and for the relief of orphans or widowes whose parents or husbands dyed in the Companies service'. The first two pensioners were installed in 1628. More almsmen followed, and in 1674 a school was educating twenty-five sons of Company servants. Prayers were read there morning and evening. After the building of a chapel near by, a chaplain was appointed – having preached a trial sermon to the approval of the local people.[7] Similarly, the Company sent chaplains to the churches and chapels in the settlements, and the 1698 Charter stipulated that there should be a chaplain on every ship of 500 tons burthen. As his life shows, Elihu Yale would have been in sympathy with the Company ethos, for he was not only a businessman but also, as his father had become, a keen churchman and a generous benefactor to good causes. John Evans, a fellow Welshman, one of the chaplains sent out to Madras, later Bishop of Bangor, became a lifelong friend.

The first hazard was the fifteen-thousand-mile-long sea voyage to Madras. Here the Company had the advantage of its own fleet of 'East Indiamen', ships built of the best English oak at the Deptford dockyard and fortified to withstand attacks from pirates and battles with the trading vessels of the Dutch, French and Portuguese. Powered only by sail, the ships had to navigate through the English Channel, across the Bay of Biscay, along the coast of Africa, with a stop at the island of St Helena, round the Cape of Good Hope, then round Cape Comorin and up the eastern side of India to reach the Coromandel Coast. What with the risk of becalming, hurricanes,[8] squalls, and accidents to the captain and crew, the journey, reckoned at a minimum of six months, could take a year.

OVERLEAF

3. The arrival at Fort St George: ships anchor far out in the bay, and flat-bottomed boats bring the passengers and cargo through the surf to the beach. The scene was still as Yale would have known it in 1672 more than a hundred years later, when the artists Thomas and William Daniell reached Madras and recorded the scene.

Beside frightening storms and the threat of enemies everywhere, the young Yale would have had to face bouts of seasickness, undrinkable water, mouldy bread, vermin, and rats which could swarm round the ship, even venturing to nibble the toenails of the sailors sleeping in their bunks. As Dr Johnson said, 'being in a ship is being in a jail, with the chance of being drowned'. Given the length and dangers of the journey, the Company distributed lemon water and oranges to prevent scurvy and supplied surgeons to deal with shaving, tooth-drawing, bloodletting and accidents, and to treat dysentery. If necessary amputations might be carried out, three men holding the patient down while the surgeon operated with the dreaded dismembering saw.[9]

Madras, to which Yale had been appointed, was the most important of the Company's settlements [5, 6], the others being Surat and Bombay (Calcutta was a later addition, founded in 1690 by Job Charnock). On arrival the ship would have anchored offshore, and Yale and fellow passengers would have been rowed through the raging surf by near-naked oarsmen on a flat-bottomed *masula* boat [3], and taken to Fort St George, where the English lived.[10] The sensation of being on dry land after so many months at sea must have been strange, as was the sight of so many 'dark faces, with white turbans and flowing robes: the trees not our trees, the very smell of the atmosphere that of a hot house, and the architecture as strange as the vegetation' [4].[11] While Yale was there Madras developed under successive governorships into a city of three hundred thousand inhabitants, in which the houses of the Indian merchants were in Black Town and those of the boatmen in Maqua Town, on the opposite side of Fort St George. As for Fort St George itself, or White Town [3, 6], the trader Charles Lockyer enthused in 1710:

OPPOSITE

4. The shock for Europeans encountering a very foreign land is evoked in this image from the Geneva edition of Jean-Baptiste Tavernier's travels in Turkey, Persia and India (1681).

Beschreibung
Der Sechs Reisen
Johann Baptista
Taverniers.
Ritters und Freyherrns
von Aubonne.
In Türckey Persien
und Indien.

J.C. Bockliner sculpsit A° 1681.

Genff.
Beÿ Johann Hermann Widerhold.
1681.

OVERLEAF

5. 'Prospect of Fort St George and Plan of the City of Madras', *c.* 1710. Strong walls surround the Fort or White Town (at the bottom). In the centre of the Fort is the Governor's House, or Fort House; to the left, the church and Town Hall. Outside to the right lies the Black Town. Top left is a view of the Fort from the sea [cf. 6]. The survey was made for Thomas Pitt [72], who was governor in Yale's last year.

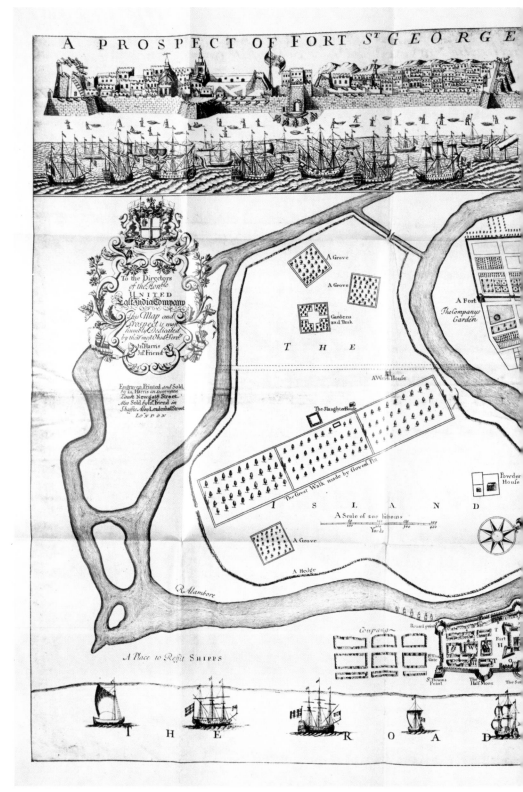

A PROSPECT OF FORT St GEORGE

To the Directors
of the Honble
UNITED
East India Company
This Map and
Prospect is most
humbly Dedicated
by their most Obedt. Servt.
John Harris
their Friend

Engraven Printed and Sold
by Jn. Harris in Brownlow
Court Newgate Street.
Also Sold by his Friend in
Shaftesberry Alley Leadenhall Street.
LONDON

A Grove

A Grove

Gardens
and Tank

A Fort
The Companys
Garden

THE

A Watch House

The Slaughter House

Powder
House

The Great Walk made by Govr. Pitt

A Scale of 200 fathoms

Yards

THE   ISLAND

A Grove

A Hedge

R. Alambore

Company

Round point

A Place to Refit SHIPPS

Fort

St Thos. Gate

St Thomas
Point

The
Half Moon

The Sea

THE   ROAD

J. Van Ryne delin.   Publish'd according

Fort St. George on the COROMANDEL *Coast.*
Belonging to the East India Company of England.

                                                Publish'd 1ᵗ May 1794 by J. M.

Le Fort Ste George sur la Cote de Coromandel.
Appartemante a la Compagnie Angloise des Indes Orientales.

.53 Fleet Street London.

The prospect it gives is most delightful: nor appears it less magnificent by Land: the great Variety of fine Buildings that gracefully overlook its Walls, affording an inexpressible Satisfaction to a curious Eye. Towards the land it is washed by a fruitful River that every November, half a Mile distant, discharges itself into the Sea, the Bar being first cut for its passage, which proceeding from the wet Monsoon, would otherwise occasion great Damage, by overflowing the adjacent country . . . The Streets are straight and wide, pav'd with Brick on each Side but the Middle is deep Sand for carts to pass in: Where are no Houses are Causeways with trees on each side to supply the Defect. These being always green render it pleasant to those who otherwise must walk in the Sun. There are five Gates – The Sea, St. Thomas, Water, Choultry and Middle Gate. The Second and Fourth may be opened for Passengers at any time of Night, if unsuspected, but neither of the other three after Six. The Publick buildings are the Town Hall, St. Mary's Church, the College, New House and Hospital with the Governor's Lodgings in the inner fort . . .

The delicious Fruits which the Country abounds with are a great help [to the inhabitants] in their Extremity: nor are they wanting to themselves in other Respects: Bathings and Wet Cloths being often applied with Success to the Relief of the Panting. It seldom lasts above four or five hours in a day: when the Sea-breeze comes on, the Town seems to be new born. The Governor, during the Hot Winds, retires to the Company's new Garden for Refreshment, which he has made a very delightful Place of a barren one. The costly Gates, lovely Bowling Green, spacious Walks, Teal-pond and Curiosities preserved in several Divisions are worthy to be admired. Lemons and grapes grow there.[12]

Trade was the reason for the existence of the society of Fort St George, which was strictly paternal in character. At its head was the governor, a person whose tough constitution had with-

ON THE PRECEDING PAGES
6. The southern and central part of Fort St George, seen from the sea [cf. 5]. On the right is the Governor's House, behind the central Sea Gate; to the left, the spire of St Mary's Church and the finialled roof of the Town Hall stand out.

stood the strain of keeping up English habits in a tropical climate and who was usually the most senior member of the governing council. He represented the British monarchy, lived in some state, and went about with an escort of English guards and eighty armed peons or footsoldiers, with two Union flags carried before him, to the sound of 'country musick' – according to Lockyer, 'enough to frighten a stranger into belief the men were mad'.[13] However, as far as the directors in London were concerned he was not a prince but the chief merchant of the settlement, whose first duty was to make profits for the Company, the second to keep good order, and the third to maintain good relations with the surrounding Indian powers. Most of his time was spent inspecting and checking native exports, preparing the annual cargoes in time for shipment before the northeast monsoon in January, and receiving and disposing of imports from Europe. Each governor was liable to dismissal with every dispatch from England, for his character and actions were freely criticized by members of the council in Madras in private letters to the directors, who, having no experience of the conditions of business in India, were only too ready to believe what they were told. This explains the turnover of governors during Yale's time there. The excellent Governor William Langhorne was replaced in 1677 by Governor Streynsham Master, who after four years' loyal and able service also lost the confidence of directors, and was followed by Governor William Gyfford. When he too was dismissed, his place was taken, very reluctantly, by Yale, who was to suffer the same fate.

Ambitious, assertive, independent, the councillors, who quarrelled frequently, were, in rising order of seniority, bookkeeper, warehouse-keeper, customer or collector of customs, mintmaster, and paymaster. The governor had no real power over them, but should an issue be undecided he was allowed a casting vote. Below the council came the senior and junior merchants, the factors, and the writers or clerks. Typically, each man who had risen through the grades to a place on the council aspired to become governor, and most plotted to get rid of the incumbent so they could rise to the top. The numerous independent merchants permitted after 1683 to reside in the Fort were headed by twelve aldermen and a mayor chosen annually. The mayor presided at the mayor's court, which tried all cases civil and criminal, with right of appeal to the governor and council. This system of justice, which made debts enforceable, attracted business people – Jews, Huguenots, Armenians – to settle in Madras rather than in the Dutch and French settlements.

Unmarried councillors resided in the Governor's House, also known as Fort House, at the centre of the Fort [5]. The others had their own houses inside the Fort, as did the Armenian and Jewish merchants and the Capuchin fathers. The factors – about eight of them – were housed in a college; they were forbidden to be out of the Fort when the gates were shut, but the rule was usually ignored.[14] The settlement was protected by a garrison consisting of 250 Europeans, 200 'topasses' or 'black mungerel Portuguese' (men of mixed race) serving as gunners [7], and 200 armed peons (footsoldiers). They lodged in the 'New House', where each had a child servant. Their main duty was to mount guard and 'see no disturbance is made in the streets through which they pass, to suppress gaming houses, to stop all people suspected to be running of goods'.[15] The garrison day began with the beat of arms at seven summoning the men to guard duty at the Main and Choultry Gates, to an occasional drill on the island, patrolling streets at night, and shutting the gates. There was time to fill, so the soldiers congregated at taverns and punch

7. A 'topas' with his wife and child, from the
account of his journeys by Johannes Nieuhof,
associated with the Dutch, then English, East
India Companies, 1682.

houses in bazaars for billiards, backgammon and gambling, while their officers speculated in trading ventures.[16]

Religion, as required by Company policy, was not neglected. In 1680 St Mary's Church was dedicated, described by Lockyer as 'equal of London except for the lack of more than one bell'. A chaplain, enjoying a precedence next to the governor, was paid the generous salary of £100, plus his diet allowance and the use of a palanquin [10]. His duties were to read public prayers thrice on Sundays, to take daily morning and evening prayers, to administer the sacrament once a month and on three major festivals, to catechize youth, and inevitably to conduct funerals as well as the occasional marriage and baptism. The Fort observed Sunday as a day apart.

> Betwixt Eight and Nine the Bell tells us that the Hour of Devotion draws near, that a whole company of above 200 soldiers is drawn out from the Inner Fort to the church door to Guard the passing President. Ladies throng to their Pews, and Gentlemen take a serious Walk in the Yard if not too hot. On the Governor's Approach the Organs strike up and continue a Welcome till he is seated, when the Minister discharges the Duty of his Function according to the Forms appointed by our prudent Ancestors of the Church of England.[17]

Medicine in Madras was in the hands of the surgeon, who was paid by his patients, and not always promptly, with the result that some had to wait so long for their money that they abandoned their profession and became traders. However, the hospital for the soldiers, sailors and lower Company servants had a good reputation, which indicates that it was usually staffed by conscientious surgeons. The most common complaints, according to one Captain Fryer in 1694, were 'Fluxes, dropsy, barbiers [a form of paralyis], scurvy, loss of the use of hands and feet, gout, stone, malignant and putrid fevers'.[18] One of the causes of illness was excessive eating and drinking, which was the main pleasure of the very restrictive life in the Fort.

The day began early, with morning prayers at six. Business was done in the offices until dinner was served at noon. Then the employees ate 'liberal fare washed down by copious draughts' at a common table over which the governor presided. Persian Shiraz and wines from Europe (among which Madeira was a special favourite), English beer, and arrack punch were drunk by everyone with 'temperance and alacrity'. The food consisted mainly of kebabs varied with 'dumpoked' fowl – boiled with butter in a small dish and stuffed with raisins and almonds – eaten with mango *achar* and sony or soy sauce. On Sundays and public feast days they might eat antelope, deer, peacock, hare, partridge, and all kinds of fruits – pistachios, plums, apricots, cherries, etc. The meal was followed by a siesta, after which some went back to the office or warehouse and the senior officials to their gardens. The evening was spent paying calls, and then, after supper again at the common table, prayers were said at eight and the gates shut at eleven.

There was no leave, no respite in hill country, and little sport except shooting, bowls, riding and coursing.[19] The few women who accompanied their husbands had to adjust to the difficult climate and the absence of the comforts taken for granted in temperate England. They were attacked by armies of white ants and mosquitoes, and, as Macaulay was to discover when he lived in Calcutta in the 1830s, the climate 'destroyed all the works of man with scarcely one exception. Steel rusts; razors lose their edge; thread decays; clothes fall to pieces; books moulder away, and drop out of their bindings; plaster cracks; timber rots; matting is in shreds.'[20]

Yale spent the years from his arrival at Fort St George in 1672 until his departure in 1699 as an employee of the East India Company, and one must ask why a man of his abilities should have chosen to pass his best years in exile under a burning sun, risking an early death through fever, for no other consideration than the low wages paid at every level. The answer is that the Company's agents were at liberty to enrich themselves through private commerce, subject to regulations. This meant that all writers, merchants, councillors and governors who lived to rise to the top of the service often accumulated considerable fortunes by trading on their own account. It was this loophole that gave Yale the opportunity to realize his ambition to live well both in India and on his eventual return home, and the incentive to stand firm when confronted by difficulties of all kinds, presented both by his colleagues and by the outside world. To achieve his ends he had the precious assets of health and a strong constitution that enabled him to continue working consistently and successfully while so many of his colleagues collapsed and died.

The proof that Yale enjoyed excellent health is provided by the minute book recording the 'consultations', for during the eleven years following his promotion to the council he did not miss a single meeting. He steadily worked his way up from the low clerical position of writer to the responsibility of assistant to John Bridger, the warehouse-keeper, in 1679. This was an exacting position. Together they received the textiles from the Indian suppliers, checking that the quality matched the sample on which the contract was given, making up the invoices so that everything was accounted for, and packing the different types of cloth into bales, which were then clearly marked and stored until ready for dispatch on the ships. Fort St George exported no fewer than fifty types of cloth; there was no uniform spelling and the names could be easily confused, so Yale must have devised his own system for distinguishing between the different weaves, textures, weights, patterns, breadth of stripes, and places of origin. The cargoes were always large. Those shipped in 1679 were as follows: 31,575 pieces of long cloth packed in 1,263 bales, 3,090 pieces of fine long cloth in 103 bales, 5,400 pieces of blue long cloth in 216 bales, 4,300 pieces of brown long cloth in 215 bales, 42,160 ordinary 'salampores' (cotton cloth, plain and dyed, usually with stripes or checks) in 527 bales, 7,680 pieces of 'betelles', 1,280 pieces of 'Moorees', superfine, and 4,160 pieces fine, 680 pieces of gingham, 840 pieces of 'dyapers', 3,040 pieces of neckcloths 16 to a piece, and 37,500 single neckcloths, red and striped. Overseeing the packing of so many items into a total of 2,519 bales, then casting the invoices that totalled 113,352 pagodas (the unit of currency), meant long and exacting work for Yale, but he took care to see that everything was entered in the books in time for approval by the council.[21] So important was the trade in silks and cottons that it overshadowed the other exports, which included saltpetre (used for the manufacture of gunpowder), pepper from the Spice Islands, Japanese screens, and Chinese ceramics.

The arrival of the ships from Europe in June was a great event, when the Sea Gate was thronged with people watching the landing of supplies and passengers. The warehouse-keeper and his assistant then had to take charge of a wide variety of European goods: broadcloth, serge, beer, sword blades, guns, coral, brimstone, paper, quill pens, iron, gold and silver bullion,[22] Norwich cloth, sponge head nails, large grindstones, chests of surgical instruments, flint stones, looking glasses, and knives. Yale had to examine and invoice all these items, and weigh the gold and the silver Spanish pieces of eight.

Another call on his time, from July 1679, was the administration of justice, at the mayor's court. In the duty of deciding appeals he was assisted by the twenty-seven law books sold by Governor Sir William Langhorne to the council for reference.[23] Yale's study of these standard texts was to stand him in good stead as he became embroiled in legal issues raised by fellow council members opposing him, and when he appointed himself chief justice of the superior court presiding over murder trials, sentencing pirates, punishing theft, etc., to the benefit of the native population of Madras.[24]

In 1680 Yale was promoted to provisional customer, an appointment that required all his bookkeeping skills. There were two sets of accounts. One covered the duties received from Indian suppliers of goods, details of house sales, slaves, etc. (Yale never owned slaves, and when he became governor he prohibited the trafficking of slaves in Madras.) The second recorded all sea and land customs received from 'Christians and Indians upon goods exported and imported', freight due to the Company for goods brought on their ships, and information about every ship anchored near by. His next, and rapid, promotion was to mint-master, in charge of coining money. As such he now joined the council. Meticulous in this new position, as always, he impressed the other councillors by bringing to their attention ingots of gold he judged to be of inferior quality. After assay his judgment was vindicated and a report sent to Sir Josiah Child in London. Soon after, Yale was given the chance to prove that he was much more than a conscientious accountant and methodical storekeeper. In December 1681 the council sent him on an important mission to Porto Novo south of Madras, close to a Danish settlement, in order to obtain a concession to trade, and in spite of bad weather, a dangerous journey, and the mystery of Oriental manners, he succeeded in his business objective, demonstrating his powers of persuasion, diplomatic skills, and, in his reports, a good command of words. On his return to Fort St George he was gratified by the sound of a salute of eleven guns fired in his honour. Soon he had the second place in the council and was now acting governor.[25]

His personal situation had changed, for in 1680, now aged thirty-one, at St Mary's Church he married Catherine Hynmers, widow of a former bookkeeper. This meant that he moved from the bachelor quarters in the dilapidated Fort House to a spacious house, and to a ready-made family, as Catherine had two children. Most importantly, the marriage gave him access to her capital, which he could now use for private trading ventures, duly registered by the provisional customer. It is the key to Yale's wealth, which was to be gained through years of successful trading, principally in precious stones: rubies, pearls, sapphires, and diamonds.

Yale's gemmological knowledge was put to the test when he was responsible for supplying three heavily jewelled girdles and seventeen elements to embellish a ceremonial umbrella for the King of Siam, set with diamonds, emeralds, and 1,256 rubies. In spite of the scarcity of faceted stones he succeeded in obtaining them, and, after checking, the finished jewels were accepted and signed for. Then followed accusations that he had overvalued the rubies, and the Siamese authorities accused him of fraud, instead of fulfilling his hopes with further commissions. Yale was soon vindicated, once it was revealed that the allegation had come from the head of the French trading company in Siam, determined to destroy the reputation of their English rivals.[26]

By dispatches arriving from London in 1687 the current governor, William Gyfford, was dismissed and Yale appointed, but although so ambitious he was reluctant to replace such an

8. The Mughal Emperor Aurangzeb in armour on horseback, *c.* 1680. In 1687 he captured Golconda, with its diamond mines.

excellent man, so unfairly dismissed. To mark his appointment he presented a handsome silver alms dish to St Mary's. He now had to face the threat of invasion from the army of the Mughal Emperor Aurangzeb [8], who had defeated the old Golconda dynasty and was advancing ever onwards, plundering and destroying local commerce, driving thousands of refugees into Madras, which was already beset by hurricanes, famine and plague. In addition to defending the Company's interests against the Great Mogul he also, with a garrison of only four or five hundred soldiers, had to be ready to withstand attacks from the French and Dutch. Every shipment from London contained letters from the Company directors demanding increased revenues, rents and duties.

Caught between two fires as he was, his powers to deal with increasingly difficult situations were diminished when the directors withdrew his authority to remove dissident council members. It was this ruling that enabled an 'enemy within', the dour Scottish lawyer William Fraser, who had arrived in 1685, systematically to destroy Yale's reputation. At first all proceeded relatively smoothly: action was taken promptly against enemy forces, security improved, new wells were dug and supplies of grain stored in case of a siege, while the business of the Fort continued; he also acquired a subsidiary trading station at Tegnapatam, which he renamed Fort St David. However, in spite of his undoubted efficiency, his relations with the other councillors deteriorated to such an extent that he was suspected of poisoning three hostile councillors, and accused of unjustly hanging the groom Charles Cross, of bribery, of avoiding payment of anchorage and freight duties, and of helping himself to the Company funds – all detailed in a closely written report of thirteen thousand words in thirty-six folio pages sent in October 1690 by William Fraser to the directors in London. Yale was placed under house arrest and replaced as governor by Nathaniel Higginson in October 1693.[27]

There is no doubt that as his intentions were increasingly frustrated by his colleagues, instead of winning them over to his point of view Yale became increasingly abrasive, domineering and arbitrary. His biographer Hiram Bingham attributed this change of attitude to the Governor's domestic circumstances. His son David died aged four in 1688, and a year later his wife Catherine took their three daughters, Catherine, Anne and Ursula, to join her two sons by her first marriage in England. It would be ten years before Yale met them again. A man of strong passions, left on his own aged forty, he engaged Hieronima, widow of the Portuguese diamond merchant Jacques de Paiva (see p. 158), as his housekeeper, and she soon became his mistress, and the mother of his son Charles, born in 1690 (Charles took his mother's maiden name, Almanza, and died in 1712). While Catherine's influence on her husband was beneficent, the relationship with Hieronima, which was contrary to the Christian morals he professed, seems to have had a damaging effect on his character.[28]

Money was another issue. As he expanded his business interests not only across India but also to new markets in Southeast Asia, China and the Philippines, and purchased at least four ships of his own, two of them named significantly the *David* and the *Diamond*, his success was resented by his colleagues. It aroused the suspicions of the directors in London, and his 'greed and avarice' were undoubtedly one of the causes of his dismissal. However, when the news came, instead of removing himself in disgrace after the appointment of Higginson, Yale remained in Fort St George, successfully defended himself against the allegations,[29] and watched the discrediting of Fraser, who had caused him so much trouble. True to form, Fraser next quarrelled with Governor Higginson, who accused him of 'a base, malicious and crafty design'; he was later suspended by Thomas Pitt [72], who after taking over in 1698 reported that Fraser had 'neither a grain of sense nor manners that ever in any way contributed to getting a penny for his employers but by his uncontrollable nonsensical obstinacy has lost them many a thousand pounds'.[30] Meanwhile, Yale was left free to pursue his profitable private interests, until he decided to return to Britain in 1699.

Although the following years of retirement reveal much about his way of life and his cultural and intellectual interests, it is his career at Fort St George that tells us about his character, brains, and abilities in dealing with all sorts of people, with the unfortunate exception of his colleagues during his years as governor. His speech was free of pedantry and pretension, and his written instructions to the commanders of the ships carrying cargoes from Fort St George are always clear and well thought-out, avoiding confusion and misunderstandings. He wrote flattering, tactful letters to the native princes, which showed not only his command of the English language but also a grasp of diplomacy that is perhaps surprising in view of his commercial background. The terminology is unfailingly courtly, and while he was careful never to give offence he stood his ground when asked to make concessions. Thus, when the powerful commander General Sadeek demanded that he hand over the unfortunate families who had taken refuge in Madras from the Mughal army, instead of refusing outright to release them, he claimed that they had gone into hiding and could not be found. Negotiating with local rulers – 'a huffing crafty people that will get what they can and omit no wayes to accomplish it'[31] – he sent valuable gifts of scarlet cloth, diamond rings, rosewater and guns to accompany his requests, emphasizing the prosperity that the Company's trade had brought to India. By these means he usually obtained permission for new settlements and trading rights on very reasonable conditions. He was fair and just to his suppliers, and the weavers of the best-quality cloths who settled with their families in Madras were provided with houses, a temple, and the music and fireworks customary at feasts, weddings and burials, all guaranteed by contract. When famine and epidemics reduced the local people in Madras to sell themselves and their children into slavery, he did all he could to prevent it. As he understood that stately etiquette and the outward display of authority impressed the Indian people, he dressed well and insisted on marking public events with due solemnity. Thus three ambassadors sent from Persia to the King of Siam were received with every sign of honour and respect, including a loan of money – which unfortunately, in spite of Yale's splendidly phrased appeals, was never reimbursed.

The accession of William and Mary in 1688 was proclaimed with bonfires, cannons and other formalities, and followed by the flying of the royal ensign over the Fort. Here Yale excelled himself by calling out the entire garrison to drink punch, and offering all the eminent residents a collation on the terrace of Fort House. The unfolding of the flag was greeted by volleys of shot, hurrahs from the crowd, salutes from the ships, the freeing of prisoners, and a distribution of money to the poor. As a stickler for order and decorum Yale ensured that the salutes of guns that greeted important visitors and messengers were made with the correct number of firings, and that the use of ceremonial umbrellas and palanquins [10, 36] was restricted to those entitled to that sign of rank. Conscious of his military duty to protect the Fort, he saw to it that visitors were greeted by the display of model artillery: a graduated set of

9. Elihu Yale would have conducted his business
in the same formal manner as this Dutch trader,
Cornelis van Bogaerde, negotiating with three
merchants *c.* 1687 – impeccably dressed, with his
sword beside him.

10. A palanquin, suspended from a curtain-tied, tasselled curved bamboo pole and carried by two or four bearers, was the means of transport for people of consequence, and the umbrella, signifying the vault of the sky, is a symbol of high rank. Yale saw to it that they were used only by the right people (including the chaplain of Fort St George).

three pairs of brass cannons, complete with carriages, nine others also with carriages, a brass gun and carriage, and five mortars for firing grenades, named after the Dutch military engineer Baron Coehorn.[32] On the walls of his consultation room he displayed groups of firearms 'curiously arranged in several figures in imitation of those in the Tower of London'.

No detail escaped him. In the interests of greater dignity he renamed the streets in the Fort from 'Points', 'Scotch' and 'French' to the more patriotic 'James', 'Charles' and 'Church'. (Back in London, this concern for questions of formality, protocol, precedence and display won him the friendship of the King's Master of the Ceremonies, Sir Charles Lodowick Cotterell: p. 48.)

As his career at Fort St George unfolded it is fascinating to see how he developed from an inexperienced young clerk knowing little of the world to assume the responsibilities of the higher grades, culminating in his appointment as governor. For Yale, as for other outstanding Englishmen in the history of British India, the long years of service to the Company provided the education and training that enabled him to rise to every challenge, as well as great opportunities to make, honestly, slowly and not easily, the money that underpinned the next phase of his life, that of a dedicated art collector, churchman and philanthropist, and his continuing activities as a dealer in diamonds.

2

LONDON
LIFE

In February 1699 Yale set out for England, taking with him five tons of valuable cargo. Hieronima Paiva and their son Charles were left behind, and so, having separated from his wife Catherine, he was now on his own. He maintained his father's country house, Plas Grono [69], and also the Manor House at Latimer in Buckinghamshire, which became the home of his estranged wife and their unmarried daughter Ursula, and settled in London, then the second largest city in Europe after Naples. In 1710–11 he bought a large and comfortable house in Queen Square (named after Queen Anne) [11, 12], one of the new developments lined with mansions in a classical style with high, well-lit rooms, and filled the large garden with statuary and plants and trees in pots. The north side of the square was left open 'for the sake of the beautiful landscape which is formed by the hills of Highgate and Hampstead'.[1] In addition, he acquired two more houses in Southampton Row near by, and a smaller third house in Brunswick Row with coach houses and stables. Neighbours included the celebrated court artist Sir Godfrey Kneller [67, 72, 122], who established his academy of painting in Great Queen Street, and the collector Dr Richard Mead, whose art gallery was attached to his home in Great Ormond Street.

It was not only good architecture that made London, the capital of a country that led the world in commerce, agriculture and politics, so attractive to a newcomer like Elihu Yale, but also the lively atmosphere. Samuel Molyneux, visiting from Ireland in 1712–13, enthused over

> the great populousness and variety of its inhabitants. You may I think in London visit Europe and meet natives of all the countrys in the world, the temperateness of its climate, makes it as easy a retirement from the

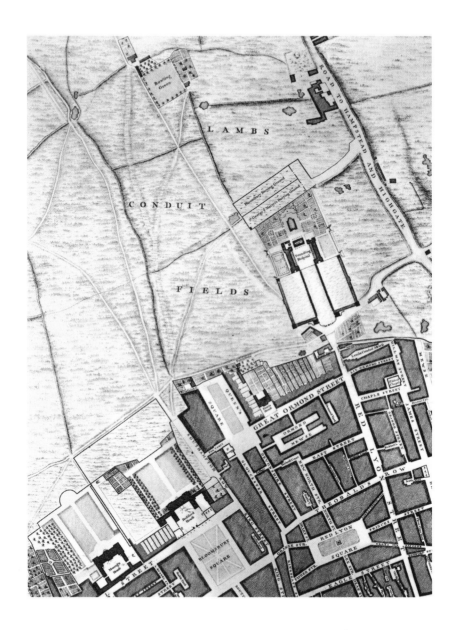

11. Queen Square, where Yale lived, appears in the centre here – a very long square, open to the country at the north. Running out of it to the right is Great Ormond Street; to the left is Southampton Row, between the built-up area and Bedford House in its grounds (now Russell Square); beyond that is Montagu House, the future British Museum.

12. View of Queen Square looking towards the
the hills of Highgate and Hampstead. At the far
left is the church of St George the Martyr [66].

sands and heats of Affrick as from the Ice and Deserts of the North, Graecians and Swedes meet in its streets and find their countrymen already settled there nor are its inhabitants in this respect less various ... here you meet the most learned men and the greatest rogues, the deepest politicians and the most trifling fops ... the great and happy liberty of England has made noblemen more than commonly civil and familiar and I must say this for the Politeness of London that I have always met since I have been here with greater Affability and Courteousness from people of the most distinguished character than I could hope from people of my sort ... Isaac Newton, Dr. Sloan [53], Mr. Halley ... the great opulency and trade of this city has unquestionably been the occasion of such large public buildings – the largeness and riches of the shops, the very signs in London are remarkably rich – Mr. Bateman is the best bookseller in whole world. The number of coaches and carts [is] also surprising, and indeed, there is no time of day you can pass the great street without meeting Carts and Coaches to stop you.[2]

The diversity of goods for sale in the shops impressed Joseph Addison, who wrote in *The Spectator* in May 1711:

Our ships are laden with the harvest of every climate: our tables are stored with spices, oils, and wines; our rooms are filled with pyramids of China, and adorned with the workmanship of Japan: our morning's draught comes to us from the remotest corners of the earth: we repair our bodies by the drugs of America and repose ourselves under Indian canopies. My friend Sir Andrew calls the vineyards of France our garden: the Spice Islands are our hotbeds: the Persians our silk-weavers and the Chinese our Potters. Nature indeed furnishes us with the bare necessaries of life, but traffic gives us a great variety of what is useful, and at the same time supplies us with everything that is convenient and ornamental.

Of all the trading enterprises that contributed to this prosperity, the most important was the East India Company, which Elihu Yale had served for many years. Starting with spices, it had gone on to change European taste, importing Indian textiles, carpets, miniature paintings, tea, coffee, and the lacquers and porcelains of China (see below, pp. 187ff.).

Wealthy individuals such as Yale were expected to stand up for themselves and protect their property at a time when riots were common, and the term 'mob' came into general use. He must also have known about the attack on the house of another East India Company official in 1697 by 'a rude multitude' of London weavers demonstrating against the importation of wrought silks by the company.[3] Criminals roamed freely, stealing from houses and shops, and pickpockets such as Daniel Defoe describes in *Moll Flanders* (1722) were active on the fashionable streets. Highwaymen both in the London area and on the roads outside held up travellers and removed any possessions of value. These circumstances account for the quantity of pistols and guns in Yale's possession (p. 88).

It seems clear that Yale must have encountered resentment of his wealth and his way of spending it, in addition to the high-handed manners and lack of tact that had alienated his colleagues at Fort St George. He was one of the earliest of a new class of Englishmen known as 'nabobs', who had acquired large fortunes in India which they displayed ostentatiously on their return home. Macaulay explained that it was 'natural that not having had the opportunity to mix with the best society the nabobs should exhibit some of the awkwardness and some of the pomposity of upstarts. It was natural, too, that during their sojourn in Asia they should have acquired some tastes and habits surprising if not disgusting to persons who had never quitted Europe.'[4]

13. Edward Harrison (1674–1732) was
appointed governor of Madras in 1711. This
wax figure shows him wearing an informal
Indian house gown and a soft nightcap over
cropped hair. Harrison acquired fine ivory-
inlaid furniture from Vizagapatam [22, 104].

Sir Charles
Lodowick Cottrell K.

14. Sir Charles Lodowick Cotterell (1654–
1710), portrayed by Michael Dahl *c.* 1690 with
his badge of office as Master of the Ceremonies
to the Court.

47

Light is thrown on Yale's London way of life in 1710 by Edward Harrison [13], then a Treasury official but soon himself to be governor of Madras, in a letter to Thomas Pitt:

> in his choultry [hall or loggia intended for transaction of public business] hid in tobacco smoak with a greasy nightgown and in a chair by him a scurvy painter or two drawing him in for some choice pieces in which he is become a very great virtuoso or a bubble [a dupe]. Sometimes you find him sett between two diamond cutters sometimes a broker or two about matching his daughters and often with the ingenious Charles Cottrell of the Ceremonies.[5]

Yale's great friendship with Sir Charles Lodowick Cotterell [14], whose official duty was to receive and entertain all foreign visitors, especially ambassadors, was based on their shared passion for formality and pomp, but the Cotterell family attributed Sir Charles's decline into melancholia and early death to Yale's 'dissolute company'.[6]

A certain reclusiveness in Yale surprised his one-time friend Sir John Chardin [55], a business partner, and as early as 1701 he wrote to his brother, the Madras diamond dealer Daniel Chardin, who himself had been associated with Yale in India (p. 151) and continued to trade with him:

> Elihu Yale first went abroad with a lackey, well dressed and living like a gentleman. Now he has greatly modified his ways and lives in a secluded manner. I now no longer go to see him at his house where I went thirty times without once being able to get him to come to my house in the country [at Turnham Green, west of London]. I found him timid, undecided, always on the defensive and, in a word, of no great consequence.[7]

Any reclusiveness is unlikely to have been on account of his class, which was by no means plebeian, for he was armigerous, owning an estate in Wales, as well as the son of a merchant. The divisions between late 17th- and early 18th-century aristocracy, landed gentry and merchants in England were neither rigid or hereditary, and individuals and families were accustomed to move up and down according to circumstances. Unlike the French nobility who formed an impenetrable caste, the English aristocracy was not exclusive. On the contrary, it was

> constantly receiving members from the people and constantly sending down members to mingle with the people. Any gentleman might become a peer, the younger son of a peer was but a gentleman ... the yeoman was not inclined to murmur at dignities to which his own children might rise and the grandee was not inclined to insult a class to which his own children might descend.[8]

Successful merchant grandees enjoyed huge influence and status. There was Sir Robert Clayton, the son of a poor farmer who had risen from scrivener's apprentice to life in a palace, described by John Evelyn. Also well known to Yale was Sir Josiah Child [15], richest of all the East India Company directors, whose wealth compared with that of the great nobles of the period. He began life sweeping the floors of a City counting house but through his abilities rose to opulence, power and fame. A baronet, he lived in a stately home at Wanstead, surrounded by magnificent parkland, 'as commonly these overgrown and suddainely monied men for the most part seate themselves', according to Evelyn. Sir Josiah married one daughter to the heir of the Duke of Beaufort, and his thirteen-year-old granddaughter to the fourteen-year-old

Wriothesley, future 2nd Duke of Bedford; the marriage turned out happily, and the young couple invested her fortune in further mercantile adventures and in building East Indiamen at Rotherhithe, the shipyard acquired by her father, John Howland, a City draper. By so easily absorbing the new rich the great families played a part in the development of the country by land and sea, since the interests of trade were as important to them as interests in land.[9]

Once they had made their money, successful merchants acquired land, the unmistakable sign of social standing. In the north, for instance, Sir William Blackett, leading merchant and mine owner on Tyneside and Whig MP for Newcastle, became a landed proprietor in the heart of rural Northumberland, having bought the estate of Sir John Fenwick, an impoverished Jacobite. In Essex, Daniel Defoe in his *Tour through the Whole Island of Great Britain* (1724–27) observed that the rich estates of Mr Western, iron merchant, and Mr Cresset, wholesale grocer, showed how 'the present increase of wealth in the City of London spreads itself into the country and plants families and fortunes who in another age will equal the families of the ancient gentry who will perhaps be bought out'. This close connection between landed and trading interests gave stability and unity to the social fabric in England that was lacking in France. Whereas the opportunities for the younger sons of the French nobility were limited to careers in the Church and army, those of the English landed gentry were much wider, at least during Yale's lifetime. Many went into trade, as one finds in the plays of William Congreve and George Farquhar. The writer of a letter to the *Gentleman's Magazine* in 1732 recalled, 'I remember and am now 73 how the younger sons of our best families were usually bound apprentices to eminent merchants.'[10]

15. Sir Josiah Child (1630–99), a formidable businessman, was a director of the East India Company almost continuously from 1674 to 1699, covering Yale's career in Madras. Under his rule it – and he – prospered, as the settlements expanded and were given military protection. Portrait by John Riley, *c.* 1680.

16. Catherine Yale with her husband, Dudley
North, and their children outside Little
Glemham Hall in Suffolk, *c.* 1715. The house
was furnished with tapestries [36], silver and
furniture from her father.

17. Lady Anne Cavendish, painted by
Jonathan Richardson the Elder *c.* 1725. The
younger of Yale's daughters had married Lord
James Cavendish [18], son of the 1st Duke of
Devonshire, in 1708.

In these circumstances Yale knew he could arrange good marriages for his daughters. As Daniel Defoe explained in *Moll Flanders*, money was the chief consideration in matchmaking: 'if a young woman have beauty, birth, breeding, wit, sense, manners, modesty and all these to an extream, yet if she have not money she's nobody . . . for nothing but money now recommends a woman.' As co-heiresses, both girls found well-born husbands. Catherine, the elder daughter, married Dudley North, eldest son of Sir Dudley North, a Turkey merchant considered one of the ablest men of his time, who lived 'splendidly and hospitably' in a mansion in Basinghall Street, and nephew of Lord Guilford, distinguished lawyer and Lord Keeper of the Great Seal. The marriage, arranged by the bridegroom's widowed mother, was a success, and the young couple 'settled in prosperity with his family at Glemham in Suffolk' [16] until her early death in 1715.[11] The other daughter, Anne [17], made an even grander marriage with Lord James Cavendish, son of the 1st Duke of Devonshire and younger brother of the 2nd Duke, greatest collector of a great collecting family – a connection also highly gratifying to Yale, himself a keen collector. A group portrait of Yale, his lawyer, Mr Tunstal, the bridegroom and his brother [18] marks the agreement to the contract by which Anne was to receive £800 annually in addition to properties in Buckinghamshire and Hertfordshire.[12]

18. Celebrating agreement on the terms of the marriage settlement between his daughter Anne and Lord James Cavendish, Yale – holding a long clay pipe – sits flanked by the Duke of Devonshire and Lord James; behind stands the lawyer, Mr Tunstal. On the table are glasses of wine, pipes, a taper, tobacco box and tobacco stopper. Lord James, too, was a collector of works of art and rare objects [87].

3

———

AT HOME

Once established, Yale lived graciously. In the house in Queen Square the wainscoted walls of the high-ceilinged rooms were covered with pictures tightly packed together and hung in tiers, and also with mirrors – chimney glasses above the coal fires in the hearths, and pier glasses between the curtained windows. The ears were charmed by the sound of music from birds in their cages, bringing a country atmosphere to London. An authentic and comprehensive view of Yale's possessions – furniture, paintings, textiles, silver, jewelry, arms, musical and scientific instruments, books, curiosities, clothing, and more – is given by the catalogues of the sales held after his death in 1721 [120, 121].

Since his London house was the setting in which Yale could entertain his social equals and superiors, the furniture distributed over his dining room, parlours and drawing room was for show – modern, comfortable and rich. There was a similar concern for comfort in the bedchamber and closets where he worked and slept. The interiors had an Anglo-Indian character, as he mixed new purchases made in London with some of the items brought home from the East.

Besides a 'Right India Cabinet' there were other 'extraordinary cabinets in great variety',[1] large and small, placed on lacquered, carved gilt wood or ebony stands, as well as oval and card 'India tables'.[2] Another important Indian speciality was ebony furniture from workshops centred on the Coromandel Coast, notably the region of Vizagapatam in the Madras Presidency, as well as from Ceylon (Sri Lanka). This wood, prized for its fine texture, jet black colour and brilliant polish, was made into distinctive designs with twisted elements, relief carving, and tortoiseshell and ivory inlays, for the European way of life. This was the source of the Yale ebony cabinets of various sizes, silver-mounted, inlaid with ivory, tortoiseshell and mother-of-pearl, and painted within.

19. This marquetry cabinet on stand
exemplifies Indo-Portuguese luxury furniture
of the type Yale brought back from India. The
pattern of trailing foliage is inspired by Mughal
decorative arts.

20. The simple form of this late 17th-century ebony table cabinet from the Deccan is enriched by the ivory inlay decorating all the drawer fronts with peacocks and hybrids between flowering plants.

21. A late 17th-century table cabinet, typical of furniture made in Vizagapatam for the European market. The rich brown mottled tints of the tortoiseshell are set off to advantage by the ivory frames.

There were also two sets of chairs (some with 'elbows'), a daybed, a bedstead, and an important inlaid dressing table, all versions of European models: such furniture was not in the Indian tradition.[3]

Throughout his long years in Fort St George Elihu Yale had been involved in the purchasing, packing into bales, and shipping of at least fifty types of cloth (see above, pp. 28–29), so it is reasonable to assume that some of the textiles in his sale were also of Indian origin, acquired there and brought home. Of the fabrics listed – dimity (ranging from fine to coarse), sprigged calico, chintzes, damask, embroidered satins and silks striped and in lively colours and printed in beautiful patterns that did not fade when washed – some were made up into curtains, upholstery, tablecloths and other furnishings. From a bedroom in Queen Square, for instance, came a 'Sattin quilt wrought with gold', that is, with the pattern embroidered in gold. This compares with the 'gilded chintz'

22. A pair of daybeds of ebony inlaid with ivory, with cane seats, from Vizagapatam. They belonged to Edward Harrison, Governor of Madras [13].

bedhangings observed on her travels in 1701–3 by Celia Fiennes in the house of Mr Rooth in Epsom: 'a bed crimson damaske lined with white India Sattin with gold and crimson flowers printed'.[4] Also from India were 54½ yards (50 metres) of 'Bed damask', 'Chince quilts lined and fringed, Fine rich Indian stich'd quilts', and silk and calico counterpanes. For the windows there were three pull-up curtains and valance of red silk, and another four pairs of curtains and two window seats all covered in white flowered damask, sold with the 'pully rods'. The patterns used were mainly floral, tree and branchwork designs, as well as all-over floral repeats, possibly combined with Indianized copies or adaptations of European models [23]. The 'Seven yards of Red damask' such as those Yale wears in a portrait [39] are unlikely to be Indian, and that may well be the case for other items, since the catalogue descriptions are rarely specific. What is certain is that he had a rich collection of Indian objects as well (see pp. 207ff.).

For the English furnishings of Queen Square Yale's return home coincided with a period of excellence in British furniture-making: the Joiners' Company declared in a petition to Parliament in 1701 that its 'members were bred up to the said art or mystery of making cabinets, scrutoirs [or 'scrutores', portable writing cabinets, from the French *escritoire*], tables, chests and all other sorts of cabinet work. They have arrived at so great a perfection as exceeds all Europe.'[5] The range of materials now included walnut (for both large and smaller pieces and as a veneer), fruitwood, ebony, princeswood, tortoiseshell and ivory, which were used for inlays and also made up into the smaller pieces – tables for tea or cards, scrutores, screens – required for a sophisticated social life, as depicted by Marcellus Laroon [25]. A new elegance came from matching tables and chairs and from the introduction of cabriole legs for stands, tables, stools and chairs, these last with taller backs.

Greater comfort and convenience were provided by easy chairs, gateleg tables for the dining room, bureau bookcases, and chests of drawers. Clocks, sculpture, caskets, boxes and porcelain ('China ware') could be displayed on Yale's many tables, while his cabinets might contain valuable objects such as amber cups, dishes, silver boxes, trinkets and watches.

The most interesting of Yale's marble tables were both inlaid with playing cards, one of them on black marble, placed on a silvered base [24]. Another pair of marble tops were displayed on 'japanned' or lacquered frames. For the fashionable taste for the exotic was not limited to porcelain, silver, textiles and screens but also extended to furniture: a group of japanned cabinets on carved gold frames, 'cloath chests', cupboards, a dressing table with drawers, writing boxes and tables for writing and for cards [26], mirror frames [27], and longcase clocks indicate Yale's liking for these status symbols of the age. His box-like 'close stools', necessary as 'places of ease-ments', were japanned black with chinoiserie decoration, and had marble seats. (For the importation of Oriental lacquer work, and the development in England of imitations, see pp. 200–204.)

This decorative japanning looked well beside the variegated golden surfaces of up-to-date, neat, light, walnut furniture: book-cases with glass doors, kneehole writing desks [284], a scrutore, looking glasses, small cupboards, and a dressing table complete with 'dressing service' consisting of cloth, comb-cases, brushes, mirrors, patchboxes, flasks, trays and containers. Much more prac-tical for storing clothes than the customary lidded chests was a 'Wallnutt tree Chest of drawers upon balls' – a set of drawers on a stand with cabriole legs on ball-and-claw feet. Much dearer than walnut, but also used as a veneer, was princeswood, reddish in colour, imported from North America and the West Indies.

23. A *palampore* of painted and dyed cotton from the Coromandel Coast, late 17th–early 18th century. The flowering tree is an Indo-Persian motif; here it is accompanied by European vases. Yale had such textiles for his bedcovers and hangings.

24. A table with a top inlaid with playing
cards similar to this one, made in London
by Italian craftsmen in 1713, was displayed
at Queen Square.

25. An evocation of polite London society
in the time of Elihu Yale: *A Dinner Party*, by
Marcellus Laroon the Younger. The room is
hung with paintings, and there is elegant silver
and glass on the table and sideboard.

26. English furniture-makers produced their own version of Oriental lacquer. These late 17th-century japanned folding tables could be used for games of chance, writing, and the drinking of coffee, tea and chocolate.

27. A veneer of Chinese lacquer, known as
'Bantam ware', on the frame gives an exotic
character to this looking glass.

28. Veneered in finely textured walnut, this versatile kneehole chest of drawers of 1715 could be used as a desk or dressing table as required.

Princeswood was described by Sir Hans Sloane in 1707 as 'a very stately tree affording very broad Boards to make tables or Cabinets making a very pleasant show, hence the name Prince's wood amongst our cabinet makers, they using it very much'.[6] Used only on the highest quality furniture [29], it was represented in the Yale collection by a 'Dolphen' table, a scrutore, and several boxes.

A few items – another scrutore, a cabinet, and some table tops – were covered in marquetry, which was much more expensive than plain veneer. This technique, of which the leading London exponent was the Dutchman Gerrit Jensen, of St Martin's Lane, involved the inlaying of thin strips of figured walnut, apple, pear, holly, box, yew, sycamore and beech to form patterns of flowers and arabesques [59]. Another small group, consisting of a tortoise-shell and ivory inlaid cabinet and a silver-mounted scrutore on a stand, was possibly influenced by the furniture of André-Charles Boulle in France, though it could also have been Indian.

The various types of furniture in the sale catalogues help to visualize the life led in Queen Square. They included sets of chessmen carved from ivory and from horn, cards, and gaming tables: card playing – picquet, whist and ombre – was obviously a great amusement, as were chess, cribbage and other games of chance. The new bookcases with glass doors housed the impressive library more effectively than curtained shelves. Round and oval gateleg tables with falling leaves meant that meals could be taken anywhere, and tea, coffee and chocolate could be enjoyed seated round one of the many examples [98]. Glass chandeliers hanging down from the ceiling, pairs of glass and silver wall sconces, and candlesticks on tables and stands brought great improvements in lighting, and the effect of the wax candles reflected in the mirrors above the chimneypiece and between the windows would have been magical. Yale's mirrors were surrounded some by deep black frames [cf. 27], others by frames of walnut, marquetry, verre églomisé (patterns in gold leaf placed between two thin sheets of glass), and gilt or silvered carved wood. Some had matching wall sconces. The most expensive was a 'Large glass in glass frame and gilt outside the top finely carved and gilt plate being 6' 3" x 3' 9"' (almost 2 x 1.15 metres), valued at £30; most of the others were valued at £4 each. The mirrors, except for the pier glasses, were hung in such a way that the frames tilted out several centimetres from the wall. No longer rarities, these expanses of glass lit up the rooms and made them seem more spacious; the long mirrors amazed those unused to seeing themselves reflected from top to toe.[7]

By the end of the 17th century the craft of upholstery had evolved so much that on entering a room it was the coverings on the seat furniture that caught the eye. Chairs, stools, and sofas with padded backs, arms and seat cushions provided a hitherto unknown degree of comfort [30]. Two easy chairs in the Yale collection were covered with black velvet, another with needlework, a sofa with yellow floral patterned silk, and an 'easy chair on casters' with Russian leather. As a further consequence of the advances in upholstery, beds were now larger, loftier, and covered in velvet or damask with curtains hanging from deep cornices, exemplified by a Yale 'Bedstead of wrought Satten lin'd with a white damask with a case and rod about 13 foot [nearly 4 metres] high' [cf. 100]. No account of seat furniture in this period could omit a most important English speciality, the light and practical cane chair with high back and crested carving [31], made in sets, with matching couches.

It says much for the excellent taste of this period that so many of the pieces of furniture that were in Queen Square could still be

29. Princeswood was the most expensive of all
cabinet woods. Yale's pieces have not been traced;
this late 17th-century table and mirror frame at
Beningbrough Hall in Yorkshire show its beauty.

30. A comfortable easy chair of *c.* 1705–10 from Chastleton House in Oxfordshire. It would have been covered with a fine textile: on two of Yale's there was black velvet, and on another, needlework.

31. A walnut cane chair of 1717, from a set at Canons Ashby in Northamptonshire.

in use today, and that the practical and elegant designs have been so frequently copied over the intervening centuries.

Throughout history silver, bright and shining, has been adopted for coinage and for articles of value, worn as jewelry, and displayed as ornaments for the table and interior. For rich men such as Elihu Yale silver symbolized social status, as did that stolen from *The Tatler's* fictitious Lady Fardingale in 1710: 'silver pot for chocolate or coffee, broad brimmed flat silver plate for sugar with Rhenish wine, silver ladle for plum porridge, silver posnet to butter eggs, two cocoa cups, ostrich's egg with feet and rims of silver, eight sweetmeat spoons, silver tobacco box with tulip engraved on the top'. Like hers, the Yale silver seems to have been acquired for everyday use as well as for display, and principally for the table.

Yale's eating habits were most likely to have been similar to those observed at the end of the 17th century by the French visitor Henri Misson:

> the English eat a great deal at dinner: they rest a while and to it again till they have quite stuffed their paunch. Their supper is moderater: Gluttons at Noon and abstinent at night . . . at dinner they will have a piece of boiled beef and then they salt it some days beforehand and besiege it with five or six heaps of cabbage carrots turnips or some other herbs and roots well peppered and salted and swimming in butter: a leg of roast or boiled mutton dish'd up with the same dainties, fowls, pigs, ox-tripes and tongues, rabbits, pigeons all well moistened with butter without larding. Two of these dishes always served up one after the other make the usual dinner of a substantial gentleman or wealthy citizen.[8]

Although from the catalogues there is no indication of whether all his silver was contemporary, and if so whether it was supplied

by the Huguenot silversmiths Paul de Lamerie, Paul Crespin and Peter Arcambo, whose technical and design innovations dominated London trade from 1700; if it was newly acquired, then French influence would certainly have been evident. As centrepieces for his table and sideboard he possessed several gilt cups, one in the shape of a pineapple, another enamelled, and a third listed in the sale catalogue as a 'Large silver cup and cover . . . new Sterling silver' – presumably one of the massive two-handled decorative designs characteristic of early 18th-century taste. For drinking beer, wine and punch there were pint mugs, tankards, flagons, bowls, dram cups, and a large 'monteith' with notched brim where drinking glasses could be placed to cool in the water [32].[9]

Since all well-regulated families drank tea in the morning and again in the afternoon [98], the Yale collection included all the items necessary for this daily ritual: silver kettle, spirit lamp and stand, a tea table, teapots, and sets of three caddies or canisters, one for green tea, the second for Bohea tea, the third for sugar. Silver

32. A silver monteith of 1689 at Erddig, the house of Yale's neighbour and friend in Wales. It is engraved with Chinese figures, reflecting the new taste in England for the Orient.

33. A silver chocolate pot, made in London
by John Fawdery in 1714/15. The finial on the
lid is hinged so the contents could be stirred
before serving.

coffee pots and chocolate pots [33] and cups reflect the popularity of both drinks, the former in a set with six cups and a syringe, the latter with a mill for grinding the chocolate to a powder. For the dining table there was an impressive array of salvers of various sizes, some executed in 'pierc'd work', a soup tureen with ladle, salt cellars, sets of sugar casters with matching dishes and spoons, plates, and baskets for cake, fruit and bread. More details are given in the sale catalogues for the dishes – pierced, finely chased, imitating basket work – and the figurative 'Fine silver chas'd dish being part of St John's Revelations at 6s. per ounce'. Saucepans, chafing dishes and plate warmers added comfort and convenience to dining. The numerous sets of silver-mounted knives, forks and spoons came with handles of amber, tortoiseshell, agate, ivory and buck's horn, and in various sizes as required for eating meat and dessert and for serving salt and sugar. For journeys to and from the estate in Wales there was a 'Compleat set of travelling plate gilt in Chagreen Case handles studs silver'.

Silver sconces, candlesticks and snuffers played a role in lighting up the rooms at Queen Square. The sconces were fixed in pairs on either side of the chimney glasses, and branched out so that the flame was reflected in the polished back plate, which might also be embossed. However, as the fashion for the drapery style of curtain brought the hazard of fire from sconces, candelabra soon took their place as the preferred means of lighting. As was the custom among keen smokers, Yale would have offered the flame from one of his candlesticks as an overture to friendship and conversation when a brother smoker visited him at home. Elsewhere in the house there was a silver writing box for his desk, and a piece of sculpture representing Cupid and a snake (the young Hercules?). A group of 16th-century Portuguese silver formerly at Madryn Castle in

North Wales, traditionally believed to have been a gift brought from India by Yale, included a silver-gilt dish embellished in the centre with the bust of a woman [34].[10]

While silver was a long-established luxury in Europe, Chinese porcelain was an exotic novelty [35]. Yale's pieces can be divided into two groups: those for display, and those for use, all presumably from the K'ang Hsi period (1662–1722). In the first category, placed on brackets, shelves, china cabinets or mantelshelves, on top of cabinets or beneath tables, come his blanc de chine porcelain figures, a cockerel, a cock, and two pairs of guardian lions of the traditional Chinese models. More numerous were his vases and containers – a punch bowl with a glass ladle, a china box, bottles, jars, one of them with a cover, two basins, and beakers large and small, all decorated in blue with pagodas, trees, bridges, mandarins and their ladies, on either white or gold grounds. For the tea table, with the silver kettle and spirit lamp, there were canisters, two candlesticks, several teapots, one in the shape of a toad, blue-and-white cups and saucers, and a set of eight japanned cups with saucers. An Oriental porcelain plate bearing the Yale arms must have been part of an armorial service commissioned for a member of the family.

A recent British innovation was Tunbridge ware, named after the fashionable watering place where it was created. Decorated with wood inlays in geometric or figurative designs, it was first made c. 1685 by a Mr Wise, from beech or sycamore. The technique intrigued Celia Fiennes, who visited the resort of Tunbridge Wells in 1697 and found the shops full of toys, silver, china, and 'all sorts of curious wooden ware, which this place is noted for[:] the delicate neate and thin ware of wood both white and Lignum vitae wood'.[11] The presence of a Tunbridge bowl in Yale's collection reflected his interest in new techniques of craftsmanship.

34. This silver-gilt dish made in Lisbon *c.* 1540 is thought to have been a gift brought from India by Yale, who presumably obtained it from Portuguese traders in Madras.

35. Yale's collection of Chinese porcelain
would have included pieces similar to those
displayed by Mary II at Hampton Court and
Kensington Palace, such as these of *c.* 1660.

By the early 18th century, carpets, which came from both India and Persia, were placed on floors rather than on tables, as had long been customary. The most expensive in the Yale collection was a 'Very fine carpet in manner of Turky work – £6. 6', boldly patterned in a few strong colours. Elihu Yale might also have brought home one of the large carpets of Persian character commissioned in India by the East India Company for European consumption.

Although only small cushions and two small tapestries were included in the sales of 1721–23, mention should be made of Yale's patronage of John Vanderbank, born in Paris, appointed Yeoman Arras Maker by William III in 1698, and the leading London maker. His tapestries commissioned by Mary II hung in Kensington Palace, on the grand staircase of Castle Howard (on the advice of the architect, Nicholas Hawksmoor), at Belton House in Lincolnshire, and in other stately homes. As the Vanderbank workshop was near by in Great Queen Street, it was easy for Yale to call and discuss the designs. His collection of Oriental screens may well have influenced the Vanderbank Indo-Chinese Soho tapestries in which the innumerable figures, buildings, exotic birds, trees and landscapes are placed on a uniform background suggesting black lacquer. A set of four panels in this light-hearted taste, new to England, was given to Yale's younger daughter, Catherine, on her marriage to Dudley North [36]. They remained in the family until sold at Sotheby's in 1924, when they were acquired for Yale University.[12] Others can be seen at Erddig near Wrexham, a house with a close connection with Elihu Yale.

In addition, Yale's house was enriched by a remarkable collection of works of art, jewels, and other objects of value (see Part II).

36. One of a set of four Soho tapestries
by John Vanderbank given by Yale to his
daughter Catherine on her marriage in 1706.
The exotic figures include a nobleman carried
in a palanquin [cf. 10].

4

GENTLEMAN OF FASHION

The sale catalogues give us a remarkable glimpse of the costume and accessories of a gentleman in the early 18th century. Since it was a time when men wore wigs over shaven heads and had smooth faces, Yale would have spent hours at his toilet table. There, attended by his servants, he had all the silver accoutrements required by a rich man: 'Dressing glasses in silver frames, chamber pots, spitting pots, shaving basins, perfume bottles, a matching ewer and basin', and 'a Large silver dressing box with 6 smaller and pincushion Case all finely chased'. In addition, ready for use was his large selection of scissors, steel and silver toothpick cases, Dutch razors (considered the best available), tortoiseshell, horn and ivory combs, and the contents of his tortoiseshell tweezer case. These things could be bought from the toymen, such as Walter Robotham [37] and George Willdey [38], shopkeepers selling, according to *The Tatler* in 1709, 'knives, combs, scissors, buckles . . . pocket books, whips, spurs, seals curiously fancied and exquisitely well cut . . . tweezer cases incomparable, you shall have one not bigger than your finger with seventeen several instruments in it, all necessary every hour of the day during the whole course of a man's life'.

Changes in men's dress, particularly the introduction of the vest, increased the number of buttons required. Sleeve buttons fastened the shirt at the wrist, and a coat had large buttons down the front and smaller buttons on the pocket flaps and on the turned-back cuffs and back pleats [40]. They were not only practical but also emphasized the cut of the coat. According to *The Tatler*, orators in the City coffee houses had the habit of twisting off the buttons of an audience: they 'get hold of them as a handle for discourse, and some are therefore argued out of several dozens'.

With the exception of a pair of sapphire buttons, which could have been Indian [cf. 110], and a set of '53 gold buttons with small

37. Trade card of Walter Robotham, *c.* 1730,
displaying seals, étuis, buckles, cane-heads,
pocket-books, cases for knives, forks and
spoons, watch chains, whips, spurs, toothpick
cases and reading glasses.

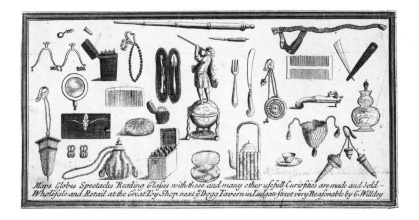

rubies on the top', the Yale buttons were relatively inexpensive, consisting of many mother-of-pearl groups each comprising four dozen, some large, some smaller, mostly set in gold, which in one case was enamelled black. A group of fourteen dozen small buttons were tipped with silver, thirteen dozen were decorated with ciphers set in gold, and eight dozen glass buttons (probably from Nottingham) were said to be 'very strong and will not break'. In addition, Yale owned no fewer than 116 pairs of buttons and studs – some silver – for his calico shirts. With his shirt he wore either a muslin neckcloth or a lace cravat with ruffles (he had a store of yards of lace for use when required). In his wardrobe were embroidered silk waistcoats, velvet caps, fine sashes, and purses of silver and silk.

Attired in his long coat worn over a shorter tightly fitting vest, knee breeches, worsted or silk stockings and gloves, shoes fastened with buckles, gold-headed cane, silk purse, fob watch, snuff box, embroidered handkerchief, rich sword belt and small sword, and a diamond ring on his finger, Elihu Yale was dressed for the part of the fashionable nabob, as shown in several portraits [1, 39, 40].

38. Trade card of George Willdey, offering 'Maps Globes Spectacles Reading Glasses ... and many other usefull Curiosities ... made and Sold Wholesale and Retail at the Great Toy shop next ye Dogg Tavern in Ludgate Street'. His shop sign, in the centre, shows Archimedes standing on a globe and looking through a telescope. 'Useful curiosities' such as the items shown here feature in the Yale sale catalogues.

39. Yale as gentleman of fashion is displayed
in this portrait and the one opposite, both
by James Worsdale, *c.* 1718. Here he wears a
fashionable sharp blue coat contrasting with
his red silk damask vest and lace cravat, with
diamond buckles on his shoes. On his little
finger is a ring set with an octahedral diamond
[cf. 80]. The young coloured attendant was not
his servant; indeed, the child's image may have
been added after the portrait was finished: such
figures were commonly included in portrayals
of successful merchants [e.g. 55].

40. In this variant, Yale is dressed in a
monochrome velvet costume, enriched by
sets of buttons. The youth with him, perhaps
his nephew and godson David Yale, is similarly
dressed. As in other portraits of Yale, there
is a view of shipping in the background.

Since aprons are listed in his wardrobe it would seem he belonged to a Masonic lodge. A lighter touch is provided by 'dress, buff coat and kettle drum', presumably for the masquerades held at Lambeth Wells, Spring Gardens and elsewhere; these were the cause of much scandal, being the occasion for 'indecorous conversation and loose conduct', and no-one was admitted unless masked and unarmed.

The extensive collection of firearms and weapons sold with the Yale collection reflects his social standing. When Daniel Defoe's Moll Flanders grew rich, and prepared to set out for a new life in America, she wanted her husband to appear 'as he really was, a very fine gentleman'. She therefore bought him 'two long good wigs, two silver hilted swords, three to four fine fowling pieces, a fine saddle with holsters for pistols very handsome with a scarlet cloak'. Essential for self defence at a time when public order was only erratically maintained, they were also important accoutrements of Yale's dress. For fighting at close quarters, pistols, in pairs, were essential [41]. When travelling, a gentleman might have the smallest pair in the pockets of his coat, a larger pair in the pockets of his greatcoat, another pair cased in the coach with him, and heavy double-barrelled horse pistols in holsters on each side of the saddle. A few, of better quality, were capped with silver or steel-mounted, one of the latter inlaid with gold. His other guns, carried by hand to be fired from the shoulder, were of the following types: bullet (firing a single bullet), staff with two locks for firing twice, magazine, wind, with the popular long-range blunderbuss, the musket (five with bayonets), fusil, and carbine.[1] Musketoons, shorter versions of the musket, with large bores, were kept in the coach ready to hand loaded with shot, in case of need. A gun with three barrels for £3, and a 'magazine gun with two barrels garnished with silver',

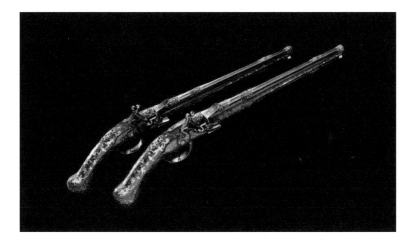

estimated at the high price of £5, were the most expensive. Their functional purpose and the absence of collector's pieces is confirmed by the generally low level of the estimates in the sale catalogues.

Very few of Yale's firearms were of foreign make. Three guns from Spain were presumably mounted with finely wrought steel, and three bullet guns and an exotically decorated 'pistol with stocks inlaid' (as well as two scimitars) were from Turkey. But during the last years of the 17th century the British gun had reached a high standard, both good-looking and accurate. This success can be attributed not only to the demands of the Duke of Marlborough for his army engaged in war with Louis XIV during the reigns of William III and of Queen Anne, but also to the existence of the Royal Society, which encouraged the science of explosives and the invention of new mechanisms. These innovations were immediately tried out by members of the aristocracy, as described by Samuel Pepys on 4 March 1664: 'several people . . . trying a new fashion gun bought by my Lord Sandwich this morning to shoot off often without trouble or danger, very pretty'. The most

41. A pair of flintlock holster pistols by Pierre Monlong, London, *c.* 1695.

expensive item in this section was to be displayed on great occasions: 'Scarlet velvet saddle embroidered with gold, housings, holsters and bags compleat @ £8 guineas'.

In addition, no gentleman could be considered well dressed unless he carried a court or small sword at his side [42]. Some of Yale's had silver grips, some were basket-hilted, and there were handles of steel, agate, mother-of-pearl, and the much rarer ebony and ivory. Many were sold complete with leather stitched belts, the more luxurious richly embroidered and fastened with silver buckles. (Yale also had a substantial range of Indian weapons: see p. 221.)

Canes, another fashionable accessory, were obtained at specialized London shops, such as that of the toyman, perfumer and snuff manufacturer Charles Lillie. According to *The Tatler* (1709), 'his canes are so finely clouded and so well made up either with gold or amber heads that I am of the opinion that it is impossible for a gentleman to walk, talk or stand as he should do without one of them.' Yale was obviously very partial to canes, possessing more than one hundred examples of different sizes. The majority of the heads or knobs were of ivory, but there were others of horn, wood, agate, tortoiseshell, and silver. Since each was different, and decorated with different motifs, they provided a talking point in society [43].

As the owner of no fewer than several hundred snuff boxes, Yale fully demonstrated his partiality for snuff and his interest in the containers designed for it. Although in use from the 17th century, it was not until 1702 that snuff assumed an important place in English social life, when British sailors, commanded by Sir George Rooke, seized fifty tons of snuff from Spanish ships at Vigo Bay and Port St Mary. Wagonloads were then sold at Portsmouth, Plymouth and Chatham for not more than 3 or 4 pence per pound.

42. The steel and gold pommel of a small sword and the top of its hilt, *c.* 1720.

43. Design for a cane head enriched with rose-cut diamonds by Marcus Gunter, 1716. Gunter was an English jewelry designer and enameller who spent the early years of the century on the Continent.

The habit quickly caught on and became firmly established in the better-class coffee houses [cf. 118]. The chief source had been Brazil, as Jonathan Swift indicates in the *Journal to Stella* in September 1710: 'I have the finest piece of Brazil tobacco that ever was born.' With the Act of Union between England and Scotland in 1707, Glasgow became the link of supply between American tobacco and the Continental market. The line 'Give the lady a pinch of sweet snuff' in *A Fine Lady's Airs*, staged in 1709 at the Theatre Royal, Drury Lane, is proof of how widespread the practice of inhaling snuff had become [98], confirmed by Lady Mary Wortley Montagu in a letter to her sister in 1723: 'making verses was as common as taking snuff'.[2]

In these circumstances the correct handling of the snuff box became an essential social accomplishment, described in an advertisement placed by Charles Lillie in *The Spectator* of 8 August 1711:

> The Exercise of the Snuff box according to the most fashionable airs and motions in opposition to the exercise of the fan will be taught with the best plain or perfumed snuff at Charles Lillie's Perfumer at the corner of Beaufort Buildings in the Strand and attendance given for the benefit of the young merchants about the Exchange for two hours every day at Noon except Saturdays at the Toyshop near Garraway's coffee house. There will be likewise taught the Ceremony of the Snuff box or rules for offering Snuff to a Stranger, a Friend or a Mistress according to the degrees of Familiarity or distance: with an explanation of the Careless, the Scornful, the Politick, and the Surly Pinch and the gestures proper to each of them. NB The undertaker does not question but in a short time to have form'd a Body of regular snuff boxes ready to make head against all the regiment of fans which have been lately disciplined and are now in motion.

44. On this most personal of all his snuff boxes, made *c.* 1710–20, Yale's portrait is pressed on the lid by the Huguenot horn and tortoiseshell worker John Obrisset.

45. Design by Marcus Gunter for a snuff box with crowned cipher ESCG, 1699. The palm of victory crossed with the olive branch of peace indicates that it was intended for a successful naval commander.

46. The Yale collection of tortoiseshell
snuff boxes included an example with the
lid decorated with flowers and leaves in the
technique of piqué-point, as in this early
18th-century example.

95

The boxes in Elihu Yale's collection provide a guide to all the designs in fashion and the range of materials used – gold, silver, tortoiseshell [44], ivory, horn, wood, amber, cornelian, agate – combining the skills of silver- and goldsmiths, painters, enamellers and jewellers. Carried in pockets lined with dimity to prevent scratching, the earliest boxes were rarely more than two inches (5 cm) in width, oval, with a tightly hinged cover. However, one of Yale's silver boxes was square, and enclosed a silver grater so he could grate his own roll of tobacco. Other shapes are listed, too: a silver snuff box in the form of a little book on a japanned table, another 'Boat fashion gilt', and a third like a tortoise. The lids were decorated usually with ciphers and heraldry [cf. 45] but also with other motifs, such as portraits of monarchs, both Charles I and George I being represented in the Yale collection, the latter carved in mother-of-pearl and the former 'in stone' (perhaps a cameo), as well as enamelled and engraved on silver. The popularity of Italian comedy is mirrored in lids of tortoiseshell boxes depicting Scaramouch and Harlequin. Unusually, a silver box lid was engraved with the pair of mythological lovers Venus and Adonis. Equally rare was Yale's 'Large round silver with limning miniature'.

Only one box was made of plain gold, estimated at a value of £3 10s. an ounce, though others were 'curiously enamelled'. The most expensive must have been 'A box set all over with diamonds', followed by 'an enamelled box set with rubies'. Most boxes were of tortoiseshell, a speciality of the Huguenot John Obrisset [44], with gold or silver mounts and studded lids, some with mother-of-pearl tops, and even several with diamonds, such as the 'Tortoiseshell snuff box, gold hinged and set with diamonds' valued at £8. Another distinctive group had designs in piqué-point, inlaid in strips or pinpoints of gold or silver in the manner of Jean Bérain, which made their appearance in England *c.* 1700 [46]. They may have been fragile, as Liselotte, Duchess of Orléans, commented when sending her aunt a small tortoiseshell box in 1714: 'C'est la plus nouvelle mode ... mais c'est une marchandise bien fragile'[3] – an opinion that Horace Walpole later underscored in a letter to George Selwyn in 1763: 'Hearts do not snap like a tortoiseshell box.' Most silver boxes were gilt inside to prevent discoloration, and one was fitted with 'a looking glass inside'. Although many were solid metal with chased or engraved decoration, some were enamelled, or combined with other materials – agate, mother-of-pearl, tortoiseshell, or crystal. In addition to the finished boxes, Elihu Yale kept a reserve of silver cast from plates and '14 fine pieces of agate' for snuff boxes.

Portrayed with his long churchwarden pipe [18], Elihu Yale evidently enjoyed smoking. He owned 3 pipe cases, 54 tobacco stoppers 'of divers sorts' to press the tobacco down into the bowl of the pipe,[4] and 54 tobacco boxes. These were made of silver, large, the lids chased, one representing the Wisdom of Solomon and another egg-shaped, with the model of a diamond, almost certainly of the famous Pitt or Regent Diamond [77]. Years later a friend inscribed a silver tobacco box, or Temple to the Goddess Nicotine, with sentiments Elihu Yale would have approved: 'Bitter cares are reduced by pleasures of tobacco, the day goes past more pleasantly, and the night flees away in a friendly fashion. You will scarcely find a friend in adversity, but here you have someone to be a friend.'[5]

5

THE PLEASURES
OF MUSIC, BOOKS,
& SCIENCE

Music the fiercest grief can charm
And fate's severest rage disarm:
Music can soften pain to ease
And make despair and madness please:
Our joys below it can improve,
And antedate the bliss above.

—Alexander Pope, *Ode on St Cecilia's Day*

The restoration of the monarchy in 1660 was followed by a fashion for musical entertainments, especially in private homes. To meet the popular demand, and attracted by the large fees offered them, Italian and German musicians flocked to London. That world is evoked by the paintings of Marcellus Laroon depicting scenes of 'relaxed informality with instrument cases and music discarded on the floor, the convivial atmosphere of tea drinking and conversation' [49].

On the evidence of his collection, Yale could have been part of the London musical scene. Not only did he possess Dutch pictures of people playing music (see p. 254) and a still life of a bagpipe, but he owned a diverse and extensive collection of instruments, some cased. These included three chamber organs, one small, one larger, and 'a fine chamber organ in a walnutt tree case and glass doors', twenty-one guitars, three French horns, two pairs of kettle and side drums, ten six-string viols and three treble viols, seven violins (one of them brass), twenty flutes, and eight English hautboys. Of his four harpsichords one was by the 17th-century Flemish makers Cornelis and Simon Hagaerts, and another, large, in a black case, by one of the Hawards, a celebrated family of keyboard instrument makers in 17th-century London [48]. Of the two others, which were in japanned cases, that valued at £7 must have been rare, since

only one of this type has survived. His three trumpet marines (a long narrow single-strung bowed instrument able to imitate the sound of the trumpet) were unusual: the *London Gazette* in 1675 had reported 'a rare concert of four trumpets marine never heard before in England'. In addition there were harps: one bell, perhaps made by John Simcock of Bath, one German, two French, and two triple harps, of a type that perhaps originated in Italy but was played by Welsh performers – echoing the Yale family origin [47].

47. The triple harp, the national instrument of Wales, played by the blind Welsh musician John Parry. He is portrayed by his son, the painter William Parry, as if lost in the sound of his own music.

ABOVE

48. This harpsichord in a marquetry case of 1683 is signed by Charles Haward, the most celebrated maker of the day. Yale's Haward harpsichord was in a black case.

OVERLEAF

49. The convivial informal atmosphere of a musical gathering at home, captured by Marcellus Laroon the Younger. One musician is seated at the harpsichord and the other plays the violin, while tea is served.

Two English curtals (a kind of bassoon instrument) and three bagpipes were described as 'not complete'. Whether for use or for decoration, he owned a chased silver trumpet. A group of flutes and two more harpsichords were described as 'old', as were a dulcimer and four citrons or cithernes (a type of guitar).

Since Yale owned at least twelve birdcages and a 'serinette', or 'instrument to teach birds', we can imagine that he also liked his house filled with their music. This is echoed by an advertisement in *The Spectator* of 11 April 1711, where a 'Widow gentlewoman, house near Bloomsbury Square' taught all sorts of birds not only to imitate human voices perfectly, but also to know the 'newest opera airs'. (Also for entertainment was a 'raree show', a portable peep-show, in which stories were acted out by small figures.)

· · · · ·

Perhaps the clearest insight into the mind and intellect of Elihu Yale is provided by the titles of the two thousand books sold from his library. Some may have been with him in India, but the most recent publications would have been acquired from the many London booksellers clustered round Paternoster Row and St Paul's Churchyard. The best known, Nathaniel Noel of Duck Lane, and Christopher Bateman at the Crown and Bible, Paternoster Row, were crowded 'every day and all day long with readers'.

These volumes on religion, geography, history, law, medicine, and Greek and Latin literature reflect his pursuit of 'enlightened learning'. They cover many aspects of Christian history and doctrine. While the *Letters and Tracts* of St Cyprian, 3rd-century Bishop of Carthage, record the days of the early Church faced with persecution, the ethical and moral problems of that time are dealt with by Tertullian in his *Works*; an 'apology' for and introduction to the new faith was given by Lactantius, the 'Christian Cicero', in seven books of *Divine Institutions* at the beginning of the 4th century, annotated by the Cambridge scholar Thomas Spark in 1684. All the key works of the Anglican Church are represented: a 'Very fine Common Prayer book in shagreen case garnished with gold', John Foxe's account of the persecution during the reign of Mary I in his *Book of Martyrs*, John Strype's *Annales of the Reformation in England* and *Life of Bishop Matthew Parker*, and Gilbert Burnet's monumental *History of the Reformation of the Church in England*, based on original documents (1679–1715). Similarly in his two-volume *Concilia, decreta, leges, constitutiones in re ecclesiarum orbis Britannici*, Sir Henry Spelman, also using genuine documents, traced Church history in England from the arrival of the first missionaries. Some of the devotional books, such as the *Sermons* of Seth Ward, Professor of Astronomy at Oxford University, Isaac Barrow's *Exposition of the Creed, Decalogue and Sacraments* (1669), and John Wilkins' *Essay towards a Real Character and a Philosophical Language*, were written by clergymen who were also founder members of the Royal Society (John Wilkins, Bishop of Chester, was its Secretary). Close to Isaac Newton was the philosopher Dr Samuel Clark, whose correspondence with Gottfried Leibniz was published in 1717, and listed in the Yale sale catalogue as 'Dr. Clark's Letters'. The most popular works were those written in beautiful prose by Jeremy Taylor: *Great Exemplar. A History of Jesus Christ* and *Rule and Exercises on Holy Living* (1650) and *Rule and Exercises on Holy Dying* (1651).

A different note is struck by the scriptural commentaries and homilies grouped in the *Works* of Jean Calvin, the influential 16th-century reformer based in Geneva. Two Latin translations of the New Testament from Switzerland in the library were popular in England, one by Theodore Beza, biographer of Calvin, the other by Johannes Buxdorf. There were also books of Calvinist theology published throughout the 17th century by three generations of the Swiss Turretin family, Benoit, François and Jean-Alphonse, who hoped to bring about the union of the Reformed and Lutheran churches. A history of the theological controversies that divided Europe for so long, the *Theses theologicae*, was compiled by Gerhard Johann Vossius. Yale kept his thinking up to date with a copy of the French Protestant Jean Le Clerc's *Harmony of the Evangelists* (1701).

The other side was not neglected. Besides copies of the Douai Bible, the Roman Missal and Breviary, the lives of the English saints, and a history of the Council of Trent, there were all twelve folios of *Annales ecclesiastici* (1588–1607), a history written in strict chronological order by Cardinal Cesare Baronius at the request of St Philip Neri. The Roman Catholic faith was also represented by a collection of eighteen Romish relics, heads, etc., two crucifixes, and Our Saviour's Nativity in a crystal case.

Another religious interest was Judaism. The earliest book was by Carolus Sigonius, *De republica Hebraeorum*, a religious, military and political history based on archival sources. It was followed by the publications of the English legal antiquary and Orientalist John Selden: *De diis Syriis* (1617) and *De synedriis et praefecturis iuridicis veterum Ebraeorum*. Yale also owned the *Works* of the English 17th-century clergyman and rabbinical scholar John Lightfoot and the *De legibus Hebraeorum* of the erudite John Spencer, a pioneering work of comparative religion, tracing the connection between Jewish religious rites and those of other Semitic peoples.

No fewer than eight hundred books written in Latin, the universal language of the educated classes, included the works of Cicero and Pliny's *Natural History*. Yale's copy of Virgil's *Aeneid* and *Georgics* was in a translation by the London bookseller John Ogilby (1663). Greek poetry was represented by the *Variorum* of Hesiod, history by the works of Herodotus, Xenophon and Polybius, and satire by Lucian's reflections on contemporary life and manners under Roman rule. A copy of the English edition of Euclid's great introduction to geometry, *Elements*, published in Oxford in 1703, demonstrates Yale's interest in mathematics and science.

Living so close to the Great Ormond Street house of the eminent physician and collector Dr Richard Mead, Yale showed his regard by buying a copy of Mead's *Mechanical Account of Poisons* (1702). In the same vein he owned Nathanael Salmon's *History of Famous Cures*, Samuel Colin's *A Systeme of Anatomy* (1685), and a portrait of the famous 17th-century physician Dr Nathan Paget.

An interest both professional and personal, dating from his career at Fort St George, is reflected in his books on the law, notably that by the great authority Hugo Grotius of Leiden University, *De jure belli et pacis* (1625), Francis Bacon's *Baconiana*, legal treatises, *Maxims of the Law* (1597) and *Reading upon the Statute of Uses* (1642), and William Beveridge's *Pandectae* on Roman law.

Earliest in the group of history books was an early printed edition of the *Chronica Majora* (*c.* 1259) written by Matthew Paris, which contains a vivid picture of St Alban's monastery. Later historical texts were John Speed's *Historie of Great Britain under the Conquests of the Romans ... to King James* (1611), Sir Richard Baker's *Chronicle of the Kings of England from the Roman Period to 1625* and William Howell's *An Institution of General History*.

OVERLEAF

50, 51. Frontispiece and title page of *L'Antiquité expliquée et représentée en figures* by Bernard de Montfaucon. The frontispiece includes temple architecture, Trajan's column, pyramids and sphinxes, vases and divinities. Yale owned the 1719 edition of this great work; it proved so popular that this second edition was issued only three years later.

Seb. le Clerc Inv. et pinxit

L'ANTIQUITÉ
EXPLIQUÉE
ET
REPRÉSENTÉE
EN FIGURES.
TOME PREMIER.
Les Dieux des Grecs & des Romains.

PREMIERE PARTIE.

Les Dieux du premier, du second & du troisiéme rang, selon l'ordre du tems.

Par Dom BERNARD DÉ MONTFAUCON

Religieux Bénédictin de la Congrégation de S. Maur.

SECONDE EDITION, REVUE ET CORRIGE'E.

A PARIS,

Chez
FLORENTIN DELAULNE,
La Veuve d'HILAIRE FOUCAULT,
MICHEL CLOUSIER,
JEAN-GEOFFROY NYON,
ETIENNE GANEAU,
NICOLAS GOSSELIN,
Et PIERRE-FRANÇOIS GIFFART.

M. DCC XXII.

AVEC PRIVILEGE DU ROY.

The most recent was the Frenchman Urbain Chevreau's *History of the World, Ecclesiastical and Civil: from the Creation to the Present Time*. There are accounts of the political struggle that dominated 17th-century England by two of the leading protagonists: William Prynne's *The Power of Parliament*, and the regicide Edmund Ludlow's *Memoirs*. A curiosity, written by the clergyman Thomas Burnet, *Sacred Theory of the Earth* (1681), suggested that at the time of the Flood the earth was crushed like an egg by the internal waters rushing out, and fragments of the shell became mountains.

Considering the amount of time and money lavished on his art collection, it is surprising to find how few books Yale possessed on the arts. These exceptions are Bernard de Montfaucon's multi-volume *L'Antiquité expliquée et représentée en figures* (1719), which laid the foundation of modern archaeological studies [50,51], a book on architecture, and Van Dyck's *Book of Heads* (the *Iconography*), complementing the many portraits in the Yale picture collection. Finally, it seems that there were manuscripts painted on vellum in the library, but no details are given in the sale catalogue.

· · · · ·

Nature and Nature's Laws lay hid in night
God said, Let Newton be! And all was light.

—Alexander Pope, intended epitaph for Sir Isaac Newton

As his library shows, Yale was a seeker after scientific knowledge, and in recognition of this he was elected to the Royal Society in 1717, proposed by the eminent physician and founder of the British Museum, Sir Hans Sloane [53]. When Henry Oldenburg, first Secretary, informed the philosopher Spinoza that the Royal Society had received its Charter in 1660, he declared his intentions: 'let us spread the sails of true knowledge, and search more deeply into the innermost parts of Nature than has been done hitherto'.[1] His hopes were abundantly realized, for under the aegis of the Royal Society momentous scientific and intellectual advances were made in England during the lifetime of Elihu Yale. The achievements of the presiding genius, Isaac Newton, in pure and applied mathematics and his formulation of the law of universal gravitation, culminating in the publication of his *Principia* in 1687, led to further hugely significant developments in the study of physics, chemistry, astronomy, and optics.

Determined to know how Nature worked, the educated public, led by Prince George, husband of Queen Anne, followed with admiration the scientific experiments of Newton and his colleagues, the Hon. Robert Boyle, Robert Hooke, John Wallis, and the Astronomer Royal John Flamsteed. Members met at three o'clock every Wednesday afternoon in rooms at Gresham College that contained a museum full of 'Egyptian mummies, old musty skeletons of men, women, monkeys, birds, beasts and fishes, a great magnet and a unicorn's horn'. There is no record of Yale attending the meetings, but the Royal Society's archives document his involvement as executor of the estate of Dr Thomas Paget: in that capacity he delivered to the Society not only bequests of Paget properties in London but also portraits of the philosophers Thomas Hobbes and Henry More and the French mathematician Pierre Gassendi.

As a member of the Royal Society, Yale collected instruments associated with the new science, made principally in London and Oxford. He may well have spent many happy hours at home in

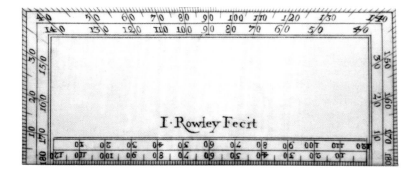

Queen Square, experimenting, testing and discussing the uses of the latest inventions, for as in the case of Sir John Chardin [55], 'it was almost necessary to the character of a fine gentleman to have something to say about telescopes and airpumps'.[2]

Essential for pursuing these scientific interests was his collection of mathematical instruments – compasses, sectors, rules, squares, dividers, protractors – of varying quality, some of brass, but other sets made from expensive ivory [52], contained in silver cases. A specialist was the London dealer Joseph Moxon, hydrographer and mathematician, author of *Mechanik Exercises* and *Mathematics made Easie* [54]. Yale's group of optical instruments – spying glasses, telescopes, camera obscuras, and a large metallic burning glass – which were obtainable from specialists such as George Willdey [38] and his partner Timothy Brandreth reflect the advances being made in the study of optics, as well as Yale's own interest in the behaviour of light. Even more numerous were his astronomical instruments, consisting of quadrants and sundials. Quadrants, invented by Edmund Gunter – graduated quarter-circles used for taking measurements, and especially for taking altitudes in astronomy – were made of brass, and Yale had both large and small sizes.

52. Rectangular protractor of ivory by John Rowley.

53. Sir Hans Sloane (1660–1753):
a terracotta bust by John Michael Rysbrack.

113

54. Illustration by Thomas Tuttell from
Joseph Moxon's *Mathematicks made
Easie*, 1705, showing globes, quadrants,
compasses, dividers, etc.

55. Sir John Chardin (1643–1712), the eminent Huguenot diamond trader, is shown here in 1700 seated in his library with a map referring to his travels (held by a young coloured attendant, a status symbol). The gilt frame decorated with scientific instruments underscores his pride in his membership of the Royal Society.

Of the various types of sundials, which were used to measure time through the fall of the sun's rays, the most expensive in his collection was the 'large universal equinoctial ring dial' estimated at £10 10s. [57]; another, of silver, was estimated at £3. Most were inexpensive brass instruments, such as a horizontal dial used to take the 'declination of walls', perhaps for making vertical sundials to fix on to walls. Yale's gunnery instruments – brass gunner's quadrants and four sets of circles for measuring the diameter of cannonballs – must date from the years spent at Fort St George, where there was always the possibility of attack from hostile forces. A barometer, or weather glass, in a 'walnut tree case' was probably displayed on the wall of one of the main rooms at Queen Square, but there were also eleven others 'of various sorts', which may have been placed for consultation elsewhere in the house. A group of surveying instruments – chains, surveying triangles, waywisers (for measuring a distance when travelling by road), and a brass semicircle – may also have been used out in India, and retained in case they should be needed on his return to London and Wales. For lifting substances of different weights he used lodestones – magnetic oxide of iron processed as a magnet[3] – of different shapes and sizes, the largest mounted in silver [58].

Supplementing his box of drugs 'for use at sea' were a large number of surgical, medical and dental instruments covering many contingencies, including amputations and cupping or draining blood, as well as four sets of 'steel instruments for cleaning the teeth' and another set 'for drawing teeth'. To complete this medicine cabinet he possessed bezoar stones [56], concretions of matter taken from the stomachs of ruminants, much sought-after as an antidote to poison, and also twelve 'snake stones' or ammonites, which were reputed to cure snake- and other deadly bites.

56. A bezoar stone and its late 17th-century
pierced silver-gilt holder on a stand. The stones
cost as much as gold on the London market,
warranting such a splendid container.

57. A universal equinoctial ring dial by Hilkiah
Bedford of Holborn Conduit, London, late
17th century. Yale made good use of this type
of instrument, and at auction his example
fetched a high price.

58. A lodestone – a form of magnet –
mounted in silver, in a mahogany stand.

In 1702 while in India, Captain Symson observed that Europeans often wore a snake stone in a gold heart hung by a gold chain from their necks, and noted that the stone was a dark, almost flat artificial stone, 'composed of ashes of certain burnt roots, mixed with a sort of Earth found at Diu', which was all re-burnt and made into a paste that hardened into a stone.[4]

Yale showed no interest in antiquarian instruments such as the astrolabe, and preferred to acquire multiple examples of the new inventions that interested him rather than assembling a comprehensive collection. There is no doubt that he was a man with a highly developed grasp of mathematical principles, very much in tune with the most advanced intellects then living in London, who, like him, as Pope's proposed epitaph for Newton (p. 110) makes clear, saw no incompatibility with religious belief.

Employed for most of his career in a trading company, Yale was inevitably interested in cartography. He was not alone. Encouraged by the Royal Society, British mapmakers produced prints, globes, charts, atlases, maps, geographical and mathematical texts and scientific instruments for travellers. All these might be bought from, among others, George Willdey and Joseph Moxon [38, 54]. Celestial and terrestrial globes, large and small, are listed, including a pair by John Senex. In acknowledgment of Yale's enthusiasm, Senex and his partner Charles Price, Geographers to Queen Anne, dedicated their new map of the Netherlands to him in 1709. There were also thirty prints and maps by Le Brun and other masters, and the works of the cartographer John Speed – *The Theatre of the Empire of Great Britain* (1611), and a series of fifty-four maps of different parts of England that appeared separately, accompanied by explanatory texts. Then in 1711 when the bookseller Moses Pitt brought out the new *English Atlas* in four volumes, elephant folio, Yale presented them to St Paul's School for the use of boarders.

Encouraged by the Royal Society, the British makers of time-keepers assumed a supremacy that was acknowledged by the rest of Europe. Thus, while travelling in Italy, both the Earl of Carlisle and Lady Mary Wortley Montagu found no present was more welcome to princes and cardinals than an English watch.[5] Living in London, the creative centre of timekeeping, Yale must have been aware of each new development. In 1675 the close interest that members of the Society took in the measurement of time, previously erratic, had led to the invention of the balance spring, followed by the adoption of the minute and second hands, which made greater accuracy in portable timekeeping possible. These discoveries were soon implemented by the professional London clockmakers, including Daniel Quare, Thomas Tompion [62, 63] and George Graham, and by others in the provinces, who created the delicate and ingenious mechanisms by hand. Immigrants also made a significant contribution. After the Revocation of the Edict of Nantes in 1685, Huguenots from the centres of Rouen, Blois and Lyon were active as both watch- and case-makers. They were not the only foreigners competing with British-born craftsmen: Zacharias Uffenbach, for instance, recorded in his *Merkwürdige Reisen* that soon after arriving in London in 1710 he went to 'the famous clockmaker Bushman – he is a German who had been established first in The Hague and then for many years in England and makes clocks as good as Quare or even Tompion whose clocks are much more expensive'.[6] City merchants and the rising middle class provided a clientèle to whom time was important and the possession of a good-quality watch essential, both on account of its function and as an enviable status symbol. Interestingly, the widespread use of watches by individuals in London was attributed by the French observer Henri Misson to the small number of public clocks there.[7]

With his usual enthusiasm, Yale acquired so many clocks and watches that he could hardly have used them all. He regarded each as a unique example of the ingenuity of the particular maker and therefore deserving of careful study. Moreover, he owned two boxes of watchmakers' tools, so he was probably capable of dissecting the movements for repair and examination with other enthusiasts. Although the portable watch predominates, he also possessed spring clocks for the table and freestanding longcase clocks, where tall boxes concealed the weights and pendulum, surmounted by the dial and movement within a glass-fronted top [59]. The design of both table and longcase clocks was influenced by the classical style of architecture, with columns and architrave, executed by cabinetmakers in walnut, marquetry, lacquer or japan, and black ebony veneer, favoured because it 'went with everything'. One of the Yale spring balance clocks was surmounted by a lion; no details are given of the appearance of the others, which indicated the hour by striking, and also the day of the month. The most notable examples listed were a 'watch piece in a walnut tree case goes 12 months' by Tompion, valued at £6, a 'spring piece in a walnut tree case' by Fromanteel,[8] and a 'day clock with several motions, a Japan case', valued at 10 guineas. Most expensive of all was a 'striking and repeating chain spring musical clock showing several motions in a tortoiseshell case', valued at £15.

Every type of watch available at the time is listed in the sale catalogues, from the plain-cased timekeeper indicating the hours and minutes only[9] through to the many elaborate pair-cased quarter-repeating watches[10] and alarm watches, even though there

59. A George I striking month-duration longcase clock by James Markwick, London, c. 1720, in a case of walnut with floral marquetry that reflects the fashion for botanical decoration.

60. A pendulum watch of 1702–3 by David
Lestourgeon, a Huguenot who arrived in
London from Rouen in 1680.

was less demand for the latter than previously.[11] Very well represented was the 'pendulum watch' with the balance visible through an aperture in the dial [60]. Competition was fierce; watchmakers, particularly the Huguenots, introduced variations, especially of dial decoration, so as to attract clients with something new. A notable example of this type was the 'sun and moon dial' [61]. Others indicated the day of the month, and there were 'wandering hour' dials and the 'six-hour dial' and 'differential dial' watch. In addition, the dial plates were enamelled and decorated with chased or engraved motifs such as foliage or trophies of arms. One piece, by Joseph Antram, 'A plain minute pendulum watch with the princess's head on the cock', indicates Yale's political loyalty to the Hanoverian monarchy.[12]

Apart from a few brass examples, all the Yale watches were made of gold or silver and would have been hallmarked, and signed by the watchmaker and occasionally by the case-maker. Paradoxically, as watches became more reliable after the invention of the balance spring, the cases housing the movement became less decorative, perhaps because they were now kept hidden, within external pair cases, as a protection from dust and accidents. The Yale inner cases were usually of circular shape, but exceptionally a silver tulip-shaped case is listed. There was one filigree case, a few were enamelled, but the majority were chased or engraved with landscapes, foliage or birds, and individualized with heraldry and ciphers. Embossed or relief figurative decoration, so characteristic of mid-18th-century watches, was unusual in Yale's lifetime. Judging from the number of examples listed, he seems to have had a great liking for tortoiseshell cases, inlaid in gold or silver with vases of flowers, foliage, birds or squirrels, a speciality of the Obrisett family, immigrants from Dieppe, and other Huguenots [62]. Also numerous were green and black leather or shagreen cases decorated with symmetrical patterns or interlaced ciphers with gold studs or pins. An expensive 'enamelled gold watch by Jolley set with diamonds' valued at £23, and two others similarly embellished and valued at 10 and 7 guineas respectively, reflect Yale's interest in jewelry and particularly in diamonds. He must have been aware of the danger posed by the many pickpockets roaming the streets of London, as described in *Moll Flanders*, so he may have been interested in the invention by Daniel Delander, who worked for Tompion, of a device attached to the outer case to prevent thefts.[13]

It is difficult to judge how many or which watches in the collection were antique 'collector's pieces'. However, as the only obvious examples of antiquarian interest were a watch 'in the compass of a ring', an 'Ancient enamelled watch', and a 'Curious enamelled gold watch' valued at £4, it would seem that he was much more fascinated by contemporary horology than by that of the past.

From the number of individual craftsmen represented in the collection it is clear that watchmaking was a business flourishing not only in London but also elsewhere in England during this period. Among the Huguenots mentioned are Paulet, Hubert, Simon de Charmes – who dealt from his aptly named premises, At the Sign of the Clock – and Henry Massy, who supplied a gold repeater with gold chain valued at £20. Besides Tompion and Quare, the many English makers include Edward East, Richard Colston [61], the brothers John and Joseph Knibb, Joseph Banks from Nottingham, John Naylor from Nantwich, and Richard Howe of Dorchester. For Yale, the nabob, these watches were more than a source of intellectual and artistic pleasure: since so many were still attached to their gold or silver chains, we can also be sure that one of his favourite occupations was deciding which one he would place in his fob pocket to be shown off in the course of his day.

61. A pair-cased verge watch by Richard
Colston of London, *c.* 1685–90. Seen through
the aperture, the gilded sun amidst clouds
alternates with a silver moon and stars.

62, 63. An early pair-cased verge watch with a
seconds hand, by Thomas Tompion, the leading
British clockmaker, 1688. The silver inner case
is by Nathaniel Delander; the outer case, of
tortoiseshell inlaid with a silver vase of flowers
surrounded by birds and squirrels, would have
come from a specialist Huguenot workshop.

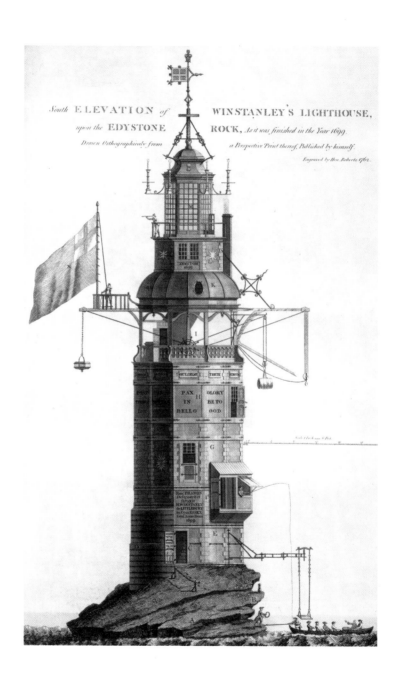

South ELEVATION of WINSTANLEY'S LIGHTHOUSE, upon the EDYSTONE ROCK, As it was finished in the Year 1699.

Drawn Orthographicaly from a Perspective Print thereof, Published by himself.

Engraved by Hen. Roberts 1762.

64. The fantastical Eddystone Lighthouse, engraved after an image published by its designer, Henry Winstanley, in 1699.

Guy Miège in his survey *The Present State of Great Britain and Ireland* (1718) considered that the 'English genius, to which they yield to no nation in Europe', was for 'the Mechanick Arts . . . and the world to this day is obliged to them for many of their useful inventions and discoveries. Here are made all the best clocks, watches, barometers, thermometers, air-pumps, all sorts of mathematical instruments, . . . and locks of iron and brass.' We can therefore be sure that the Yale padlocks and locks for doors and for strongboxes, iron chests and trunks functioned perfectly and looked good. Only size and materials are specified, except for those of the best quality, described as 'Beautiful pierced brass and blued steel work locks'.

The Yale collection included a model of one of the great achievements of contemporary engineering, the Eddystone Lighthouse, built on rocks 14 miles (23 km) off the coast of Plymouth. The work, begun by Henry Winstanley in 1695 and finished in 1698, was a highly ornamented pagoda-like structure with galleries and projections [64]. Damage by storms required further work, completed in 1700; but the force of the sea against the rocks during a great storm in 1703 caused the lighthouse to collapse, and Winstanley, who had spent the night there, was killed. John Gay recalled the disaster:

So when fam'd Eddystone's far shooting Ray,
That led the Sailor through the stormy Way,
Was from its rocky Roots by Billows torn,
And the high Turret in the Whirlwind borne,
Fleets bulg'd their Sides against the craggy Land,
And pitchy Ruines blacken'd all the Strand.[14]

6

PHILANTHROPIST

When another Fellow of the Royal Society, the diarist John Evelyn, wrote in 1685 that 'the Church of England is certainly of all the Christian professions on earth the most Primitive, Apostolical and excellent', Yale would have agreed. As the descendant of Thomas Yale, Chancellor to Archbishop Matthew Parker, one of the architects of the English Reformation, and great-grandson of David Yale, Vicar General to Bishop Lloyd of Chester, his Anglican roots went deep. He had constantly affirmed his faith while in India. Writing in 1689 to prisoners of the King of Kandy in Ceylon (Sri Lanka) on whose behalf he had interceded with the ruler, he advises them, should his plea be unsuccessful, to accept their fate with Christian resignation: 'if the Almighty is not soe pleased then pray rest contented and praise him for your lives and healths and provide for eternity.'[1] Again, he instructs the captain of one of his ships about to sail to China: 'This your chiefest duty is to give all due reverence and worship to Almighty God and keep his Sabbaths holy without whose blessing there is neither safety nor success to the greatest forces and the best designs.'[2]

On his return to England he would have been pleased to find these religious views in tune with opinion in London, where the Established Church, having come through the sectarian turmoil of the 17th century, was experiencing a revival. New churches were built, Sunday was strictly observed as a day of rest from labour, hospitals and charity schools were established, and two important organizations, the Society for Promoting Christian Knowledge and the Society for the Propagation of the Gospel in Foreign Parts [65], were founded. The chief object of these societies was the diffusion of Bibles, prayer books and religious literature to country districts at home and across the seas. They also supported charity schools where the poor were taught to read and educated in the

65. Seal of the Society for the Propagation of the Gospel in Foreign Parts. The device is of a ship in full sail, with a minister standing on the prow with an open Bible in his hand, making towards land where people await him, with the words TRANSIENS ADJUVA NOS (Come over and help us). This is bordered by the Latin name of the Society and the date of its foundation, 1701.

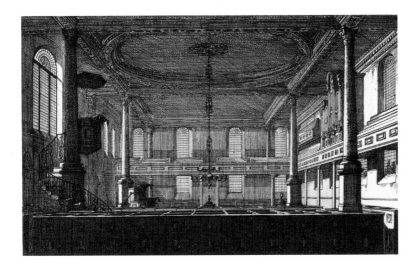

moral principles of the Church of England. Joseph Addison in the *Guardian* in 1713 applauded 'this institution of charity schools ... the glory of the age we live in, and the most proper means that can be made use of to recover it out of its present degeneracy and depravation of manners'.

Yale used his wealth to support all these causes. Elected a member of the Society for the Propagation of the Gospel in 1717, he promised to give one hundred guineas for the purchase of a building to house the records and for meetings, with room for a chapel, a charity school and library, plus £10 annually towards its maintenance. In addition he bought books for the library and promised another annual subscription of £20. No sooner had he settled in Queen Square in 1711 than he bought a pew in the new local chapel, St George the Martyr [12, 66], where he attached himself with such enthusiasm that in 1717 he was elected a trustee of the parish, and treasurer of the charity school, so that he could ensure that the accounts were properly kept.

66. St George the Martyr in Queen Square [12].
Yale knew one of the founders, Sir Streynsham
Master: Governor of Fort St George in 1677–81,
Sir Streynsham gave the church the same name,
that of the patron saint of England.

This commitment to religious and charitable causes attracted the attention of Jeremy Dummer, a lawyer acting as the London agent for the Massachusetts Bay Colony, on the other side of the Atlantic. Accordingly, Dummer wrote on 22 May 1711 to his friend the Rev. James Pierpont, trustee of the fledgling Connecticut Collegiate School in New Haven, informing him that Elihu Yale, having no son of his own, was considering making his heir a relation who lived in New Haven, and also giving money to an Oxford college. He proposed that a 'proper letter' from the Rev. Pierpont might persuade Yale, who was born in New England, to give financial support to a Connecticut institution established on the lines of an English university, 'a place wherein youth may be instructed in the arts and sciences, who through the blessing of Almighty God may be fitted for public employment both in church and civil state'.

At first Dummer went about collecting books for the Collegiate School library and received donations from Isaac Newton (a copy of his *Principia*), Sir Hans Sloane, Sir Richard Blackmore, Richard Steele, and members of the Society for the Propagation of the Gospel, including Yale, who presented the largest number, totalling 32 books, in 1713. In this he was encouraged by Francis Nicholson, who as Lieutenant-Governor of Virginia had overseen the founding of William and Mary College, and when Governor of Maryland had also furthered educational causes. As a leading member of the Society, Governor Nicholson, like Yale, believed that the right kind of books would promote the doctrines of the Church of England and educate the clergy to defend it against Dissenters. In 1716 the Collegiate School trustees began building in New Haven; they came to need further funds to complete the work and pay the salaries of the teachers, and the influential

Rev. Cotton Mather from Boston appealed directly to Yale on 14 February 1718. Reminding him of his New England connections, and the Christian character of the teaching at the college, he proposed that if it 'might wear the name of Yale College, it would be better than a name of sons and daughters. And your munificence might easily obtain for you such a commemoration and perpetuation of your valuable name, which would indeed be better than an Egyptian pyramid.'[3] Encouraged by Governor Nicholson, Yale responded to this appeal on 11 June 1718 by sending a consignment consisting of two trunks of Indian textiles to be sold for the benefit of the college, 417 printed books for the library, a portrait of George I by Sir Godfrey Kneller [67], and an escutcheon with the Royal Arms. The books mirrored his own spiritual, cultural and scientific interests, for although the largest proportion was theological – sermons by the great 17th-century preachers, catechisms, Biblical history and commentaries – there were also works on commerce, botany, trees, ancient and modern history, philosophy, medicine, travel, government, and the law.[4]

As expectations at New Haven were pitched high for more benefactions to follow, in 1718 the institution was named Yale College. Although he made promises of an annual subsidy and other gifts, Yale was getting old, and he must have felt there were more pressing demands on his purse, especially the Society for the Propagation of the Gospel. The last consignment – half of what had been promised to the indefatigable Jeremy Dummer – was sent in February 1721, a few months before Yale died. His heirs successfully contested the will and the College never received a bequest of £500. Yet his support, the largest gift from an individual donor until 1837, came at the right time. It gave the trustees the confidence to proceed with establishing what would become a world-famous

67. Yale gave the Connecticut Collegiate
School in New Haven this official image
of George I by Sir Godfrey Kneller, showing
the King in robes of state. In the same year,
1718, the School became Yale College.

university [140], training men and, from 1892, women for the highest political, judicial and professional offices. Mather was right to compare it to a pyramid.

Wales was another beneficiary of his generosity. To the end of his life Yale remained close to his Welsh roots, returning often to Plas Grono [69] (sadly the house was demolished in 1876). The journey cannot have been easy: the roads were in a terrible condition with mud everywhere, his carriage always likely to be overturned, and travel was therefore restricted to the hours of daylight. However, he was not daunted by this, nor by the threat of highwaymen, and having made the long journey from London to his country house near Wrexham, surrounded by stables, kennels, dogs and horses, Yale could enjoy the sporting rights of the squirearchy, well protected by the Game Laws. The majority of his twenty 'fowling pieces' or shotguns with long single barrels for shooting game – pheasants, partridges, duck, snipe, bitterns, ruffs, reeves, plovers – were steel-mounted except for two with brass barrels. They were between 5 and 6½ feet (1.5–2 metres) long, as it was widely believed that the longer the barrel the more effective the weapon [68].[5]

In recognition of his attachment to 'the land of his fathers' he was appointed High Sheriff for Denbighshire in 1704. He made gifts to Wrexham Parish Church where his parents were buried [70, 71], subscribed to the publication of a Welsh prayer book in 1711, and provided for a charity school in his will. The establishment of this school, like others in Wales, was to have a far-reaching influence, as the pupils were taught to read the Welsh Bible, and thus the language was preserved from destruction, to be expressed in patriotic poetry and prose.[6] Yale's strong national sentiment was expressed by his devotion to St David.

OPPOSITE
68. Flintlock breech-loading sporting
gun by Jacques Gorgo, 1690. Yale used this
type of gun with a very long single barrel for
shooting game when staying at Plas Grono.

69. Plas Grono, the Yale family house in
Denbighshire, before its demolition in 1876.
Once here Yale could enjoy the sporting life
with his dogs, and participate in local activities,
proud of his Welsh roots.

70. Yale presented these wrought-iron chancel gates, with their gilded ornament made by the local smith Robert Davies *c.* 1707, to his parish church of St Giles in Wrexham.

71. A 17th-century Italian painting of King David playing the harp, also given to Wrexham Church by Yale. For the Welsh this had a special significance: their patron saint was named David, their emblem was the harp, and they knew the importance of King David in Biblical history.

He named his first son, one of his ships, and the Company settlement he founded on the Coromandel Coast after the national saint of Wales. He wore a diamond leek symbolizing his Welsh origin in his hat on St David's Day, 1 March, following an old custom, and presented Wrexham Church with a painting of King David, psalmist and founder of the Temple liturgy [71], shown playing the harp. There were two Welsh harps in the Yale collection of musical instruments (p. 100), and they are likely to have been played to accompany the singing of traditional Welsh songs passed down in his family. Significantly too, the Welsh banker and jeweller Sir Stephen Evans was one of his closest friends, signing the marriage contract of Yale's daughter Anne with Lord James Cavendish in 1708, while a portrait by Sir Godfrey Kneller of Sir John Wynn, 5th Baronet, of Wynnstay, one of the largest landowners in Wales, was sold with the Yale paintings [121].

Elihu Yale's will begins with an uncompromising declaration of his belief:

> First being a Christian and an unworthy Member and Son of the Church of England, as by Law established, which I hope God will prosper and increase to the World's end, and so I humbly recommend my soul to God that gave it relying on his Gracious Mercy and the Meritorious Blood and Death of my dear Saviour and redeemer the Lord Jesus Christ for a free pardon and forgiveness for my Great and many sins of Omission and Commission.

The number of bequests is impressive: £200 for the poor of Wrexham parish, and outside Wales £100 each to Christ's Hospital, the hospitals of St Thomas and St Bartholomew and the

workhouse in Bishopsgate Street in London, charitable schools
for the poor, and the Society for the Propagation of the Gospel
in Foreign Parts. Then followed a list of the individuals to whom
money was left – excluding Catherine Yale, 'my wicked wife',
whose name was crossed out.

PART II

———

DEALER & COLLECTOR
IN LONDON

1

A FORTUNE
FROM JEWELS

. . . un diamant beau et parfait est le vray soleil d'entre les autres pierres précieuses.

—Robert de Berquen, *Les Merveilles des Indes Orientales*, 1669

The major part of Yale's fortune derived from diamonds, the most precious and beautiful of all stones, and his trading activities provide fascinating insights into the market for these stones, how they were mined and acquired in India, exported, and finally sold in Europe. Through the enterprise of the employees and the wise decisions of the directors, the East India Company succeeded in establishing London as the centre of the lucrative diamond trade, previously dominated by the Portuguese and then by the Dutch, and Yale's involvement continued there, for far from retiring he carried on as a successful dealer in diamonds. Hundreds of diamond rings, crosses and brooches were listed in the sale catalogues and dispersed after his death by the auctioneer Christopher Cock. Further proof of his continuing involvement is provided by his relations with Governor Thomas Pitt [72], who in 1701 sent him from Madras a large diamond weighing 45 carats, and in 1718 a bulse (a special secure purse: see below) of diamonds. The two men were friends, as well as business partners, and in 1707 Pitt wrote to thank Yale for his 'noble present of a fine silver watch and seales, two pieces of drugget and a choice canary bird'.[1]

The diamond had always been prized for its hardness and resistance to fire and anvil, but during the 17th century the progress made in cutting that released its brilliance resulted in its adoption by society as the ultimate symbol of wealth and status. Until the discovery of mines in Brazil *c.* 1725, India was the main source of these stones, esteemed for their grand *éclat*, extreme whiteness, and limpidity, known as 'purity of water'. As demand increased in the last

decades of the century production was intensified, and, seeing the rewards obtainable, from his position at Fort St George Yale became a dealer, with the reputation of a strong buyer who didn't haggle. He was one of the few who had both expertise and capital, for since the stones were useless until faceted and well polished, money laid out on them was inevitably locked up for long periods, three years being the average time taken to get a return on the original investment.[2]

Since Yale left few records of his dealing, the best guide to this exclusively Indian trade comes from the accounts of Jean-Baptiste Tavernier [4, 73], *Les Six Voyages de Jean-Baptiste Tavernier en Turquie, en Perse, et aux Indes* (1676), and of Sir John Chardin [55], *The Travels of Sir John Chardin into Persia and the East Indies* (1681). Chardin[3] collaborated with Yale, as did his brother Daniel, an East India merchant who lived in Madras for twenty-two years; Daniel acted as Yale's intermediary at the diamond mines on the east side of the Deccan plateau, centred on Golconda [75], and settled any difficulties presented by Mughal officials. This was by no means easy, as he reported in a letter from Hyderabad dated 27 February 1688: 'The trading doth continue dead as it was, or not att all. Diamonds very few. Merchants also. There is no hope to make a set of the emeralds because they that did cutt stones are dead.'[4]

Buying in this way, through a Madras merchant, was far less trouble, although more expensive, than at the markets of Golconda and Hyderabad, because the journey in palanquin or carriage required a retinue of forty or fifty armed men as a protection against robbers, and to escape the heat the distances were covered only during the night. Thanks to Tavernier, we know how the diamonds were extracted, either from rocks or riverbeds in the various mines. From 1687 these were part of the Mughal empire, and the largest stones (10–13 carats) and royalties were due to the

72. Yale's friend Thomas Pitt (1653–1726), 'Diamond Pitt', shown with a maritime background evoking his time in Madras, 1698–1707. He is well dressed, and the brim of his hat on the table beside him is fastened with a diamond button, alluding to his career as a trader in precious stones. (He acquired what became the famous Regent Diamond [77].)

Emperor Aurangzeb [8]. The methods were primitive, and each mine was different. At Raolconda and Kollur work started after dinner: using hooked rods, the men dug into the veins of the rocks for earth or sand that might contain diamonds; softened with water, this was then carried off by women and children, dried in the sun, and sifted until the stones emerged. Soumelpour was the most ancient and smallest mine; there the diamonds were found in the sand of the bed of the River Koel in February, when the level was at its lowest.

Tavernier describes how the rough stones might then be given to diamond cutters using steel wheels, though for fear of reducing the weight the shaping was minimal, as was the polishing. He observed, too, that instead of scrutinizing a rough stone for flaws, or judging the 'water' by daylight, as in Europe, the Indians did so at night, placing a lamp with a large wick in a hole excavated in a wall and judging the quality as they let the light pass through the stone held in the fingers – a method later adopted in Europe. To be quite certain of the quality of the water they examined stones under a leafy tree, for in the green shadow it was easy to detect whether the water was bluish or not. This was important, since there was a huge difference between the price of a perfect stone and one less so.

When ready, the hereditary masters of the mines, the banians or 'Braminies' (not Brahmins, but from the *bania* or merchant community of Gujarat) would bring the stones to the buyers waiting in lodgings, always giving time – even a week – for a proper examination. Time and caution were necessary, for in Thomas Pitt's opinion 'wee all know that they are Rogues enough and studdy nothing else but cheating'.[5] If the decision was 'yes', then the transaction took place immediately, and payment was made with a bill of exchange for Agra, Golconda, Visapour or Surat, with interest being charged on any delays. In the case of no sale, the diamonds were put back

73. Jean-Baptiste Tavernier (1605–89),
portrayed by Nicolas de Largillière in the
Oriental dress given to him by the Shah
of Persia in 1665.

in the seller's waistband, turban or shirt and not seen again unless mixed with others. The banian might then return with another parcel for the buyer's appraisal. If a good price had been paid for the first parcel, it encouraged the seller to show even more precious goods. Appearances were deceptive, for Tavernier noted that the worst-dressed, least prepossessing-looking banian might produce fine stones very cautiously, 'en cachette et en y joignant un air de mystère' (secretly and with an air of mystery) – secrecy being the rule: between themselves the Indians transacted business in silence and by hand, a method that intrigued Tavernier. He describes how

> the buyer and the seller sit one before the other like two tailors, and the one of the two opening his girdle, the seller takes the right hand of the purchaser, and covers his own hand and that with his girdle, under which, in the presence of many merchants who meet in the same hall, the bargain is secretly driven without the knowledge of any person. For then the purchaser nor seller speak neither with their mouths or their eyes, but only with the hand as thus. When the seller takes the purchaser by the whole hand, that signifies a thousand and as often as he squeezes it he means so many thousand pagods or Roupies, according to the money in question.

ABOVE
74. This vignette shows two Indian dealers in precious stones displaying their wares on the ground in the customary manner that Yale would have recognized.

OPPOSITE
75. Detail of a map of India drawn by Tavernier, showing the diamond mines inland from the Coromandel Coast – Golconda (between 'GR' and the word 'Coste'), and Raolconda and Kollur ('Coulour') to the southwest.

Lahor

multan

Pi

Ganges R.

Delj... janabad

ch... ...

AGRA

Ha...labas

Visapour Gemini R.

DV Gua ltor Gata m.

ladona colasav

Banavou

MO
Be

boye Amadabat

chalaou Sivonge

Patna

...oli

Di

D

Baroche

Souali

Surate Damon Bargaut

chitpour Branpour

nabout

Casimbazar Ogli

Orixa

A

Bacaim Auroougabat

N

Bombaye

chaou

Dabou ingrele

Goa

GR

Visapour Bagnagar oui

Golconda

Coste Masapour supatan

Coste de Coyomandel

Coste de

Cananor

Raolconda...

coutour

Carn

Ondicheri

Gandicou

Calicut

Cochin

Malabar

Travancor

Tanavas mas auas

O

Jafanapatan

Candy

cap Comorin
Colombo

Ponte
de Galle

I. de Ceylan

Les maldives

des

Les

If he takes but half to the knuckle of the middle finger that's as much as to say fifty. The small end of the finger to the first knuckle signifies ten. When he grasps five fingers it signifies five hundred, if but one finger, one hundred. This is the mystery the Indians use in driving their bargains. And many times it happens that in the same place where there are several people one and the same parcel shall be sold seven or eight times over and no person know that it was sold in that manner every time.[6]

Similarly, the children of the merchants, who were trained in valuations from a very early age, remained silent when they were purchasing diamonds. Tavernier was impressed by a group aged from ten to sixteen, each boy carrying diamond weights hanging from one side in a little bag, and on the other his purse with five or six hundred gold pagodas in it, sitting under a tree in the square at Soumelpour ready to buy from anyone who wanted to sell. Beginning with the oldest or 'chief', the stones offered were passed for examination from hand to hand, with not a word spoken. On the second time round the chief would ask the price, and conclude the deal. In the evening all the purchases made in this way were counted up, the stones classified according to water, weight and clarity, priced accordingly, and carried for sale to the wholesale merchants. The profit was then divided among all the children, the chief receiving more, or – should there be a loss – less than others.[7]

The process did not change, and what happened next can be taken from the description given one hundred years later by George Fox, historian of the great London jewellers Rundell, Bridge and Rundell, referring especially to the bulses, or purses:

> ... rough diamonds are taken from the mine without having anything done to them in the way of either cutting or polishing. A considerable quantity

of these having been obtained by the Native Merchant are very carefully sorted out and weighed in the most exact manner an invoice of them is then made out in which any of the stones weighing more than four grains are described separately and those that are four grains or under are put into parcels according to their respective size and described and weighed together. The whole of the diamonds are packed up in cotton cloth and made up into a parcel in shape like a round ball with a neck to it. The size of these bulses vary but generally they may be said to be about the size of a small fish. The neck of the Packet is then very securely bound with tape and the Seal (generally a very large one engraved with the owner's name etc. in Native characters) is then applied to the fastening of the tape. The Merchant, when he finds a purchaser produces the Bulse thus sealed up and exhibits the invoice he has made out of the contents and the purchase takes place without the buyer having the least opportunity of examining the contents. These Bulses often pass through twenty or thirty hands before they reach Europe, each seller affixing his seal as a guarantee that the contents are correct according to the invoice and it ought to be stated that of all the Bulses that came into the possession of Rundell, Bridge and Rundell not one of them was found to be mis-described in the Invoice that accompanied them from the East Indies.[8]

Having acquired their rough diamonds in Golconda, the merchants then brought them to the ports. In Madras, for instance, they might sell to the passengers and crew of the ships in the fleet of the East India Company, to professional dealers, and to officials like Yale with money to invest. The trade was now dominated by England. This development resulted from the decision of the East India Company in 1664 to end their monopoly and to permit outsiders to trade in precious stones, albeit subject to their regulations, which coincided with the settlement in London of Portuguese-Jewish merchants, free to practise their religion there. They brought their financial and gemmological skills to the business, which was organized on a professional basis for the first time. These merchants exported silver, coloured stones, amber and coral and imported rough diamonds, which were then forwarded to Amsterdam for cutting and polishing. This done, a proportion of the diamonds came back to London, where they were sold to jewellers. Through the expertise of the Portuguese-Jewish community, London became the centre of the international diamond trade, as a petition to the East India Company in 1695 declared: 'the business formerly driven by way of Italy or Portugal is now become almost a sole English trade'.[9]

From 1680 Jewish traders were allowed to settle in Fort St George, and one of the earliest to do so, in 1684, was the Portuguese Jacques de Paiva, financed by a London syndicate. On his death in 1687, his widow Hieronima, who became Yale's mistress, continued to trade in association with her brother, Joseph Almanza.[10]

The hazards of diamond trading from the moment of leaving India were such that it was thought only because the English were such great risk-takers did it appeal to them more than to any other nation. There was far more to the business than a good eye and judgment. The ships might sink, or on arrival in Europe the stones might be stolen by highwaymen, and after the further expenses of cutting and polishing they were not always easy to sell. A stable political situation was essential, as Philip Masson, a Parisian jewel-ler, explained to Sir Richard Hoare: 'in order to sell diamonds people must be at their ease, money must circulate and trade must be settled there must be as 'twere, a superfluity'.[11] One method was by public auction, though this ran the risk of the possible purchas-ers combining into a ring to keep the prices down.[12] Good timing was equally necessary.

Governor Pitt encountered great difficulties in 1701 in disposing of his truly magnificent flawless diamond weighing 426 carats in its uncut state. He had acquired the stone at the request of the banker/jeweller Sir Stephen Evans (also a friend of Yale's), who seems to have regretted so doing, for in reply to the news that Pitt intended sending it with his son to Europe, Evans urged caution on account of the war of the Spanish Succession. In August 1702 he wrote: 'We are now gott in a war the French king has his hands and heart full soe he can't buy such a stone there is noe Prince in Europe can buy itt soe would advise you not to meddle in it for the interest yearly would come to a great sum of money to be dead [i.e. idle] as for the diamonds received per Dutchess [a ship] can't sell them for a 8s a pagoda.'[13]

Notwithstanding the lack of encouragement, the diamond was brought to London, where it was cut and polished into a cushion-shaped brilliant weighing 140.64 carats [77]. The fame of this great treasure stirred patriotic feelings, and people, not wishing to see it acquired by the kings of France or Spain, hoped that it would adorn the English crown. Yet even at the time of the Union with Scotland in 1707 no steps were taken to mark the event with the acquisition of the best and biggest of all diamonds. It was still unsold in 1710, when Lady Wentworth, a loyal monarchist and a peeress in her own right, wrote 'for all the great Scarceity of money yet hear it will be a glorious show on the Queen's birthday: wonderful rich cloaths preparing for it there was one that see Mr. Pits great dyamant that I writ you word of and they say it is as big as a great egg: I would have the city of London bye it and make a present for the Queen's crown.'[14]

The problem with Pitt's diamond was that being so much bigger and more perfect than any other stone ever on the market it was difficult to determine its value. Moreover, the war with France and the resulting uncertainties made any prospective buyer cautious.

76. The Regent Diamond is displayed in the foreground in the hilt of Napoleon's sword of office as First Consul in 1802, in his portrait by Antoine Gros.

77. The Regent or Pitt Diamond, a cushion-shaped brilliant-cut stone some 1¼ inches (3 cm) wide. Acquired from Thomas Pitt by the Regent of France, Philippe d'Orléans, in 1717, and named after him, this diamond, on account of its size and superb quality, is the most valuable stone in the French State collection.

Eventually in 1717 it was sold, at far less than its true value, to the Duke of Orléans, Regent of France, who renamed it after himself. (It was set in the French royal crowns and then in the sword of Napoleon [76], and today it can be seen in the Louvre.) The sale made Pitt's family rich. As long as the diamond was in his possession he had had to change his name and place of residence many times when in London for fear of being attacked or murdered.[15]

For smaller stones the home market was good. According to the Swiss enameller André Rouquet, writing in the mid-18th century, the English had a marked preference for diamonds rather than coloured stones: 'they are richer, less variegated and less liable to imitation'.[16] As they were so eminently suited to the display of wealth and status, demand increased with every court event: coronations, royal marriages, the return of the King from Hanover, his birthday celebrations, recuperation from illness. However, they were always difficult to dispose of independently, as Lady Mary Wortley Montagu discovered when she wrote to her sister, who was in Paris attending the coronation of the infant Louis XV in July 1722: 'I beg you would let me hear soon from you and particularly if the approaching Coronation raises the price of diamonds. I have some to sell and cannot dispose of 'em here.' Two years later, in December 1724, she asked again: 'Now the Money is so high at Paris I wish you would be so good to enquire for what I could sell a Di'mond, clean and thick, Indian Cut, weighing 39 grains strong.' The reply was discouraging: 'This is the worst time to think of selling anything here. Money is so Scarce that I question whether anybody coud be found to buy such a diamond as you speak of. Ev'ry thing is very dear which makes people retrench their expence to what is absolutely necessary, and jewells you know cannot be comprehended under that head.' Lady Mary, disappointed, replied that 'till a fit Occasion of disposing of some superfluous Di'monds I shall remain in this sinfull Sea Cole town' (i.e. London).[17]

Elihu Yale succeeded in this risky business because he had suffi- cient capital to survive severe setbacks, such as the bankruptcy and suicide of Sir Stephen Evans, and could afford to wait to get a good price. He was also closely connected with the Portuguese-Jewish dealers, and always settled his debts with them, thereby proving that foreigners investing in diamonds through the East India Company settlements could expect to recover money owed, encouraging the diamond dealers to continue trading.[18] In the course of the century the retail jewellers organized the trade so as to keep prices high and stable, and raised the diamond 'by exaggerated praises above any fine stones to an unconscionable price'.[19]

• • • • •

Full in the midst proud Fame's imperial seat
With jewels blazed, magnificently great;
The vivid em'ralds there revive the eye,
The flaming rubies show their sanguine dye,
Bright azure rays from lively sapphires stream,
And lucid amber casts a golden gleam.

— Alexander Pope, *The Temple of Fame*

During his years in India Yale invested heavily in precious stones and pearls, as these not only made his fortune but also provided the easiest means of repatriating it. He therefore arrived home with an important stock that he sold on the London market. He had the stones cut, polished, and set in European designs.

78. Yale's strongbox for his most valuable
stones and jewels, of brass-mounted
kingwood parquetry, rests on an elaborately
carved and gilt stand. With a handle on
each side, it could be lifted up and carried
from place to place as required.

79. The interior of the strongbox, lined with
rosewood, is ingeniously fitted out with trays
and drawers so that the diamonds, coloured
stones and pearls were easily accessible.

80. A point-cut diamond – the stone in its natural octahedral form – set in a gold ring, *c.* 1600. Yale is shown wearing such a ring [39, 40].

Most of the five hundred rings that Yale owned at his death were set with diamonds, both white and fancy coloured – rose red, yellow, brown – and in a variety of cuts. The earliest, with the pyramidal point cut, described as 'diamonds to write on glass', were similar to rings used for writing names, messages and verses on drinking glasses [80]. This custom was practised by a literary gentleman noted by *The Spectator* in November 1711, who 'By the help of a very fine diamond which he wore on his little finger was a considerable poet upon glass'. In *Moll Flanders,* the suitor of the eponymous heroine 'pulls off his diamond ring and writes upon the glass of the sash, You I love and You alone, whereupon she borrows his ring to write underneath, And so in Love says everyone', and they continue the dialogue by these means until he tires of it and calls for pen and ink. Jonathan Swift, in *On Seeing Verses Written upon Windows in Inns*, complained how 'The glass, by lovers nonsense blurr'd /Dims and obscures our sight'.

81. The first step in the evolution of diamond faceting: the table cut, obtained by slicing the point from the pyramid-shaped octahedron. Table-cut diamonds in a gold ring with indented collets, *c.* 1660.

82. The rose-cut diamond, seen here in a gold ring of *c.* 1660, represents the next stage in the evolution of faceting. It was valued not only as a sign of wealth and social standing but also as a love token.

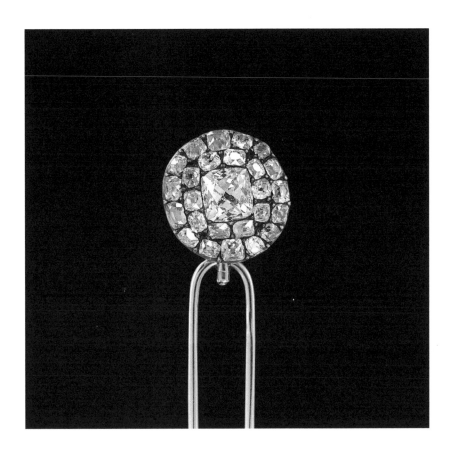

83. Early examples of the brilliant
cut, which released more fire and light
than before. Given by Charles II to his
mistress, Nell Gwynn, they were mounted
c. 1680 in a hairpin bearing her name.

The first step in the evolution of faceting is represented by rings set with flat table diamonds [81], such as a 'Yellow diamond table ring' and a 'large and fine deep table diamond ring'; this was followed by rose-cut or 'faucet' diamonds [82] and culminated in the brilliant cut [83, 84], first recorded in the reign of Charles II in the 1670s when Christian, Countess of Devonshire, acquired a 'diamond cut eight square'.[20] A Yale 'Round ring 23 small brilliant sparks set in silver' clearly indicates that by this date silver settings [84, 88] were supplanting the traditional gold, which cast yellow reflections over the white brilliance.

The larger stones were set as solitaires in oblong, oval or round bezels; the smaller were arranged in clusters [85], such as the 'diamond ring consisting of one large and six lesser' – the standard 17th-century setting of three or four stones on each side of a larger central stone. The number of stones clustered together in other

84. This fine ring set with a brilliant-cut diamond was given by Queen Mary II in 1691 to Godard van Reede, created Earl of Athlone. Yale's diamond solitaires would have been set like this in silver bezels.

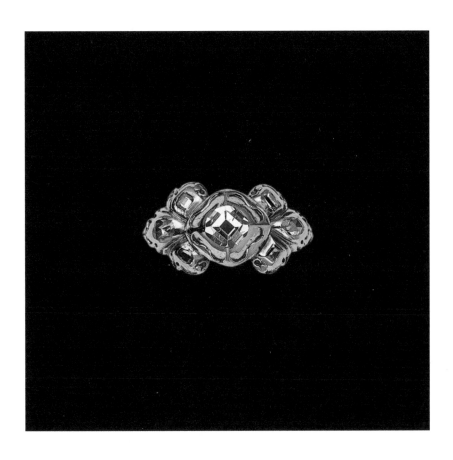

85. Seven-stone table-diamond cluster set
in a gold ring with indented collets, *c.* 1660.

groupings varied from nine to as many as twenty-three, some set side by side across the wide bezel. The smaller diamonds might be different in colour from the larger, such as white surrounding yellow.

Two rings set with engraved diamonds, one with a shield of arms, the other 'a ring with a curious head cut in a diamond', were extraordinarily rare. Hardest of all gemstones, the diamond had resisted attempts to engrave it until the 16th century, when, according to Paolo Morigia in *La nobiltà di Milano* (1595), the famous Jacopo da Trezzo succeeded in doing so, while employed in Spain by Philip II. Several 17th-century English and Danish monarchs recognized the prestige attached to the possession of a diamond signet, and two commissioned by Charles I as Prince of Wales and as King are now in the collection of Her Majesty Queen Elizabeth II. Earliest is a ring with a shield-shaped diamond engraved with his badge and initials CP (Charles, Prince of Wales); the other, with a lozenge-shaped diamond engraved with the coat of arms of his Queen, Henrietta Maria [86], could be that for which Francis Walwyn was paid £267 in 1629 'for cutting and finishing of the royal arms in a diamond and the letters of the name of our dearest consort the Queen on each side'. Dispersed during the Civil War, it emerged as the 'fine and valuable table diamond ring with arms of England and Scotland' sold from Yale's collection by Christopher Cock on 8 March 1722 as the signet of Mary Queen of Scots. (This mistaken identification reflects the influence of Jacobite loyalists, who venerated objects associated with the Stuart dynasty, and particularly with that ill-fated queen.) The signet was bought at the Yale sale by the 8th Earl of Pembroke – statesman, man of taste, friend of Sir Andrew Fountaine and of Robert Harley. In the 19th century the antiquarian C. D. Fortnum acquired it from the estate of the Duke of Brunswick and presented it to

86. One of the most remarkable jewels in Yale's collection: the signet ring of Queen Henrietta Maria. The diamond intaglio of the royal arms and initials HMR was probably engraved by Francis Walwyn in 1629. The ring disappeared during the Civil War; Yale found it in India. It was long believed to be the ring of Mary Queen of Scots.

Queen Victoria in 1887 to mark the fiftieth anniversary of her accession, having established, after ten years' tenacious research, that the original owner was Queen Henrietta Maria.

As for Yale's 'ring with a curious head cut in a diamond', this type of rarity is mentioned by Lorenz Natter, a gem engraver, who had seen most of the collections of Europe and discussed diamond engraving somewhat critically:

> Je sais par expérience que cela est fort possible aiant gravé moi-même un Vase sur un petit Diamant pour Mylord Jacques Cavendisch de Londres. Je suis persuadé que je pourrois également y graver un Portrait; non sans beaucoup de patience et autant de tems qu'il en faudroit pour le graver sur une douzaine de pierres Orientales. Mais un tel ouvrage monteroit a un si haut prix qu'il n'y a guère d'Artiste qui voulut l'entreprendre par pure curiosité et sans un ordre exprès de quelque riche Seigneur.[21]

(It is certainly possible to do this, as I know from experience, having engraved a vase on a small diamond here in London for Lord James Cavendish [87]. I am sure that I could also produce a [diamond] intaglio portrait, but this would take as much of my time and patience as to do it on twelve other hardstones. Such a task would be so expensive that no artist would undertake it out of curiosity and without a commission from a rich patron.) That Lord James Cavendish, himself a collector, married to Anne Yale, commissioned this engraved gem from Natter indicates that he shared his father-in-law's interests and tastes.

As for Yale's numerous coloured stones – emeralds, rubies, and semi-precious turquoise, garnet and amethyst – except for turquoise, these were faceted and almost all bordered with white diamonds to enhance their tint, though exceptionally a 'large bluish sapphire

87. The diamond engraved with a classical urn in this ring was commissioned from Lorenz Natter by Lord James Cavendish [18], the husband of Anne Yale. (The setting is later.)

88. White enamelled hands offer a crowned heart in this silver ring of *c.* 1700, set with rose-cut diamonds. Yale owned diamond rings of sentiment such as this, of a type used at weddings.

ring' was set with two emeralds. In addition to his two engraved diamonds, Yale also owned another rarity, a sapphire intaglio representing a head, unfortunately not identified in the sale catalogue.

Besides these decorative rings, Elihu Yale possessed others of less intrinsic value, signifying sentiment and his political loyalties. Sentiment was expressed symbolically by rose-cut diamond and ruby hearts, some offered by a pair of hands [88], others inscribed with the interlaced initials of the lovers, and by two gimmel rings: 'Hand and heart opening ring, enamelled hands one rose diamond, and 9 sparks'. These were called gimmel, meaning twin, since they were composed of two hoops representing two lovers, side by side. Another pair enclosed hair, set under glass in one and beneath a yellow diamond in the other. Support for William III was expressed by a ring with the cipher WR beneath a table-cut diamond, and for his successor, Queen Anne, by portrait rings, one crowned, the other flanked by diamonds.

Another group is set with hardstones engraved as intaglios and cameos. An early intriguing 'ring of King Henry the Eighth' was either an intaglio portrait or a royal coat of arms as used by highly placed servants to seal contracts and business documents on the Tudor monarch's behalf. Other signet rings, contemporary or earlier, are not listed, although any one of Yale's extensive collection of intaglios set in rings could have been employed for this purpose if he so wished. However, two rings set with cameo heads of young black men [89] reflect the custom of employing them as pages in well-to-do households as well as a taste for the exotic.

Earrings were naturally included in a collection of this importance. Surprisingly, there was only one pair with pear pearl drops attached to diamond tops; the others were almost all set with

89. The 'blackamoor' was a favourite theme of gem engraving from the Renaissance through the 18th century. In this ring of *c.* 1730 his exotic looks are enhanced by a diamond turban, aigrette and collar.

177

coloured stones – amethysts, emeralds, rubies – or with diamonds, both white and fancy yellow. The rose-cut diamonds were set in small clusters just covering the lobe, and also in two girandole-type pendants [90, 92]: one with 'three drops consisting of seven rose diamonds each' and a less elaborate 'Pair earrings fine rose diamonds two tops two drops'. Unspecified coloured stones were set in the same pendant styles: 'Pair green earrings with three green drops each', and 'one pair of red single drops and two white drops'. The tops might be joined to the drops by ribbon bowknots.

For necklaces pearls, large, round and flawless, enjoyed a prestige eclipsing all other gems, and there were hundreds in the Yale collection, as short chokers, multi-rowed, and chains, the pearls 'Oriental white' – with only one seed pearl example. They were fastened at the back of the neck by ribbon ties. Next in importance were his diamond necklaces. The improvement in faceting and polishing meant that the effect of a neck encircled with rays of light in a rivière was so much admired that all wealthy women wanted one [92]. Among necklaces, in addition two chains are listed: one consisted of 41 carved wooden beads, the other of 132 amethysts.

Large and small buckles were part of dress, and those in the Yale collection were intended for both men and women. They range from pairs of gold buckles set with diamonds to cheaper silver and paste versions. Only four pairs of shoe buckles are described as being specifically for men, of which there was one with pearls. Some of the buckles fastening women's gowns, stays, girdles, glove strings, hat bands and shoes were set with rose-cut diamonds or brilliants, but they were outnumbered by those with crystal stones. The most valuable were the 'Girdle buckle and necklace of emeralds', the 'Pair Buckle Diamond gold and rubie', and a 'Pair large rose diamond buckles set in gold'.

90. Necklace and three-drop girandole
earrings, of rose-cut diamonds set in silver
(the stones in the necklace separated by small
spacers), c. 1700. Yale owned examples of both
types of jewel.

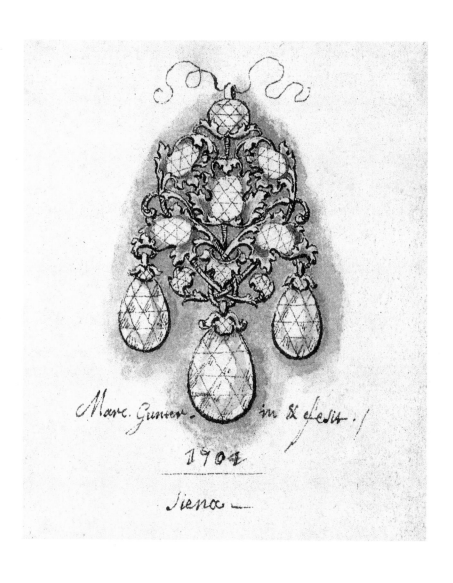

91. Design by Marcus Gunter for a rose-diamond girandole earring, 1704. He sets the diamonds amidst acanthus leaves and hangs three briolettes below. Catching the light with every movement of the head, diamond girandoles lit up the features of the wearer.

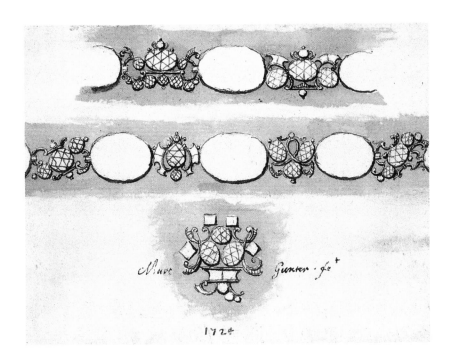

92. Designs by Marcus Gunter for necklaces
and a small brooch, 1724. The pearls or oval-
shaped gems in the two necklace designs are
separated by rose-cut diamond spacers, all
different. The brooch seems to represent a
stylized vase of flowers.

93. This pair of silver vases of flowers, set throughout with rose- and table-cut diamonds, *c.* 1710, correspond to the 'boucket' of diamonds in the Yale collection.

94. Centred on a musician playing the harp
seated beneath flowers and fruit, with birds
flying above and animals at his feet, this mid-
17th-century brooch could resemble Yale's
'Orpheus enamelled and set with diamonds'.

95. The head of a man in this jewel of *c.* 1580, his helmet set with a baroque pearl crowned with feathers, with a diamond chin strap and breastplate, suggests Yale's 'Head of a Knight Templar in gold garnished with diamonds and a very large pearl'.

Lockets, named after the tiny latch that secured the hinged cover, were very fashionable. Those in the Yale collection were enamelled, or of plain gold, 'of divers sorts', set with pearls, with diamonds, rubies or sapphires, and with square-cut blue and red stones. Sentiment was symbolically expressed by 'The hand in hand enamelled locket set with diamonds', and by a memorial locket enamelled with a 'Death's head and phoenix'. Another had two gold figures on a diamond ground. Perhaps the most valuable was the 'Gold locket of a gentleman's head set in rubies'.

Other pieces included five diamond crosses and a sixth set with rubies, one diamond and two pearl drops. A 'Watch hook', a shield-shaped plaque studded with fifty-eight diamonds, could be hooked over the girdle and hung not only with the watch but also with the key, a seal, and trinkets, such as the 'trinket for a watch set in gold with rubies, pearls and rose diamonds' estimated at £12. There were several large brooches: an 'Enamelled nose gay of 8 rose diamonds in flowers and other stones', a 'Boucket of flowers set with diamonds' [93], an 'Orpheus enamelled and set with diamonds' [94], a 'Circle consisting of 15 diamonds and 15 rubies', and an hourglass with diamonds, perhaps a pendant. Surprisingly, given the extent of the collection, few bracelets are listed: the exceptions are two pairs with matching necklaces, one set with moss agates and the other with rubies and sapphires. Two designs incorporated unusually shaped baroque pearls: 'a large pearl rising out of its shell' and the 'Head of a Knight Templar in gold garnished with diamonds and a very large pearl' [95].

2

THE NEW
WESTERN TASTE
FOR THE EAST

Strait then I'll dress, and take my wonted Range,

To *India*-Shops, *Motteux*'s, or the *Change*;

Where the Tall Jar erects his costly Pride,

With antique Shapes, in *China*'s Azure dy'd:

There, careless lies the rich *Brocade*, unroll'd;

Here, shines a Cabinet with Burnish'd Gold . . .

— Anon., 1716

Yale returned to London in 1699 with a large collection of goods acquired in India, packed within his five tons of cargo. Some pieces were displayed in the house in Queen Square, including objects that still formed part of his collection when he died (as we shall see), but he must have hoped to make a profit on others. By that date the huge success of the East India Company in importing Indian textiles, carpets, miniature paintings, tea, coffee, arrack, rice, cloves, nutmegs, mangoes in pots, and the lacquers and porcelains of China had altered the drinking, social customs, dress and artistic habits of an increasing number of well-to-do English people. Already in July 1664 John Evelyn had observed that

the East India ships brought to London such a Collection of rarities as in my life I had not seene: the chiefe things were very large, Rhinoceros's hornes, Glorious Vests, wrought and embrodered on cloth of Gold, but with such lively colours, as for splendour and vividnesse we have nothing in Europe approaches: a Girdill studdied with achats [agates] and balast rubies of greate value and size, also knives of so keene edge as one could not touch them, nor was the mettal of our Couler but more pale & livid: Fans like our Ladyes use, but much larger and with long handles curiously carved and filled with Chineze characters:

OVERLEAF

96. On a painted fan, *c.* 1680–1700, the artist has depicted the wide range of goods intended for the European market in a merchant's shop in a Southeast Asian trading station. There is an abundance of lacquered furniture – cabinets, firescreens, stands, tea-tables – as well as embroidered hangings, paintings and porcelain.

A sort of Paper very broad thin, and fine like abortive parchment and exquisitely polished of an amber yellow, exceeding glorious & pretty to looke on . . . also prints of Landskips, of their Idols, Saints, Pagoods, of most ougly Serpentine monstruous and hideous shapes to which they paie devotion: Pictures of men and countries rarely painted on a sort of gumm'd Calico transparant as glass, also Flowers, Trees, Beasts, birds etc. excellently wrought in a kind of sleve silk very natural.[1]

His interest aroused, in 1676 Evelyn 'Went with Mrs. Godolphin and my wife to Blackwall to see some Indian curiosities', and in 1683 after visiting the Whitehall Palace apartments of the Duchess of Portsmouth, the French mistress of Charles II, he noted that they were full of 'Japan cabinets, Skreens'.[2]

By the turn of the century the homes of the aristocracy were similarly furnished, and at the Duke of Bedford's London house [11] and Woburn Abbey almost every room contained something from India or China or both. There were firescreens, stands, tea tables, embroidered hangings and counterpanes from India, plus porcelain, wallpaper and other goods from China; the young 2nd Duchess of Bedford at Woburn offered to buy such items on behalf of her sister-in-law, the future Duchess of Rutland, for she kept a very close eye on the cargoes arriving on the East India Company ships, as well as attending the periodical sales held in the Company courthouse in Leadenhall Street.[3]

Indian artefacts were also acquired from shops such as those of Henry Tombes and of Peter Motteux [99] in Leadenhall Street, near 'Old India House' [2]. The latter – referred to in the epigraph above – advertised in *The Spectator* in January 1712 that he bought and imported 'rich Brocades, Dutch Atlasses [silk satin manufactured in the East] with Gold and Silver or without, and other

97. Samuel Scott depicts two ships at the old
East India Quay on the Thames, sails unfurled,
ready to leave for the East. On the quay a
merchant, wearing a tricorne hat and close-
fitting coat, takes notes while talking to sailors.
Workmen prepare bales of merchandise, barrels
and baskets ready for transport.

98. Seated at a tea-table, in high-backed chairs,
two ladies and an officer in this scene of *c.* 1715
drink tea from Chinese export porcelain cups
on saucers. The lady in the centre takes a pinch
of snuff from the officer's box.

foreign Silks of the newest Modes and best Fabricks, fine Flanders Lace, Linnens and Pictures at the best Hand'. The fashionable success of these importers was resented in some quarters, and on their behalf John Polloxfen complained in his *Discourse on Trade, Coyn and Paper Credit* (1697), 'As ill weeds grow apace so these manufactured Goods from India meet with such a kind reception that from the greatest gallants to the meanest cookmaids nothing was thought so fit to adorn their persons as the fabric of India nor for the ornament of Chambers like India.'

Before the potters of Dresden in Europe had discovered the formula for making porcelain – white, vitrified and translucent – this luxury was imported in quantities from China by the East India Company. Soon after the Restoration of 1660, another mistress of Charles II, the Duchess of Cleveland, amassed a collection of Chinese porcelain – it came to be known as 'china' – in London that was sold in Paris in 1678,[4] but the decisive influence was Queen Mary II, who amused herself at Hampton Court with forming a vast collection of seven hundred and eight pots painted with 'hideous images, and vases on which [there are] houses, trees, bridges, mandarins in outrageous defiance of all the laws of perspective' [35].[5] The taste for china spread fast, both for tea drinking [98] and for decoration, since, like silver, it signified status and an appreciation of the finer things in life. A collection displayed in a fashionable interior was described in the library of the learned 'Leonora', a Miss Shepherd, by *The Spectator* of 12 April 1711:

> At the End of the Folios (which were finely bound and gilt) were great Jars of China placed one above the other in a very noble piece of Architecture. The Quartos were separated from the Octavos by a pile of smaller Vessels

which rose in a delightful Pyramid. The Octavos were bounded by Tea
Dishes of all Shapes Colours and Sizes which were so disposed on a
wooden Frame that they looked like one continued Pillar indented with the
finest Strokes of Sculpture and stained with the greatest Variety of Dyes . . .

In a few years almost every great house in the kingdom contained
these 'grotesque baubles', and distinguished statesmen and generals
were not ashamed to be renowned as judges of teapots and dragons.
Alexander Pope and Joseph Addison mocked the fine lady who
'valued her mottled green pottery quite as much as she valued her
monkey and much more than she valued her husband',[6] but the
brilliant bluestocking Lady Mary Wortley Montagu did not agree
with the satirists, and declared that 'Old china is below nobody's
taste since it has been the Duke of Argyle's whose understanding
has never been doubted either by his Freinds or enemies'.[7]

The popularity of brilliant and long-lasting Indian coloured
textiles in Persia was noted as early as the 5th century BC by the Greek
physician Ktesias, and this traditional mastery was maintained
over the following millennia.[8] Recognizing this, the Company's
biggest success was textiles – Indian chintz dress and furnishing
fabrics and Chinese painted and embroidered silks – which by
1664 accounted for 75 per cent of the entire export trade from
India.[9] From Leadenhall Street the Company sent precise instructions specifying the colours and patterns required, disregarding
time lag and distance. Again the fashion was adopted by Queen
Mary. Celia Fiennes, riding sidesaddle across England in the
reign of William III 'to discover the nature of the land and the
genius of its inhabitants', visited Windsor and saw in the Queen's
'Chamber of State all Indian Embroidery being presented to
her by the Company on it is great plumes of white feathers'.[10]

ABOVE

99. Giovanni Antonio Pellegrini's sketch of the dealer Peter Motteux and his family in 1710 shows the lively setting of a man who arrived in London from France in 1685 and became the leading dealer in Oriental imports from his shop, At the Sign of Two Fans.

OVERLEAF

100. The State Bedroom at Erddig, the house of Yale's neighbour Joshua Edisbury, contains a six-panelled Coromandel screen probably given by Yale and Chinese bed hangings that he is likely to have supplied. The painted red lacquer cabinet is a brilliant example of English 'japanning'.

On another journey in the reign of Queen Anne, at Lady Donegall's near Epsom in 1703, Celia Fiennes noted the bed hung with 'crimson damaske lined with white Indian satin with gold and crimson flowers printed', and at that of her daughter-in-law Mrs Rooth 'a pladd bed lined with Indian calicoe and an Indian carpet on the bed'.[11] At their London house in 1706 the new beds for the Duke and Duchess of Bedford were hung with Indian damask trimmed with green silk lace.[12] A rare survival from the early years of the century can still be seen at Erddig, the house next to Plas Grono: the state bed is hung with a cream and yellow Chinese fabric [100], which is likely to have been brought back from the East by Yale.

The most outstanding example of such interior decoration was at Wanstead, the country house of the wealthy East India Company director Sir Josiah Child [15] rebuilt by his son, Sir Richard Child, which in 1724 was described as having many Indian calicoes both on beds and as hangings.[13] However, most of the cloth imported was not the deluxe painted chintzes and embroideries for fashionable homes such as these, but ordinary patterned cloths that could be bought by a wide range of people who appreciated the clear, pretty colours, the small scale of the motifs, and the sense of fantasy.

The desire to possess imported fabrics extended to men's and women's clothing, a fashion that had begun by 1661 when Samuel Pepys bought 'an India gown for myself' and two years later 'a very noble part-coloured Indian gown' for his wife.[14] John Evelyn records a visit on 30 August 1680 to Sir John Chardin [55] at his country house in Turnham Green near London, where he found Sir John dressed in his Eastern habit. It caught on so fast that in 1694 the East India Company directors informed Yale in Fort St

101. A hanging of painted and dyed cotton
from Gujarat, *c.* 1700. The chintz, which hung
at Ashburnham Place in Sussex, still retains
the brilliance of the original colours.

George that 'the greatest ladyes will now weare chintzes for upper garments as well as for petticoats. They can never make nor you send us too many of them.'[15] The variety of expensive textiles on sale in London can be deduced from Peter Motteux's advertisement (see pp. 190–93). While the fashionable 'stately fops admire themselves better in an Indian dressing gown than in one made at Spitalfields'[16] [102], people of modest means wore Indian cotton underwear and other items of clothing, 'moved to it as well for the cheapness, as the Lightness of the cloth and the Gaiety of the colours'.[17]

Worried for their livelihoods, the textile manufacturers of Spitalfields, Norwich, Yorkshire and Wiltshire considered 'Indian silks shawls injurious to them, whereas the Spices were harmless, saltpetre acceptable, but that the taste for textile imports meant that English drapery lay unsold in warehouses until devoured by moths', and called for Parliament to pass 'An Act for the Restraining the Wearing of all Wrought Silks Bengals Dyed Printed or Stained Calicoes'; appealing to patriotic feelings, they regretted the displacement of the Arras hangings of lordly Tudor mansions by painted hangings and deplored the sight of Englishmen, whose ancestors had worn stuffs made by English workmen from English sheep, now flaunting calico shirts and silk stockings from India.[18] Yet all attempts to protect the local industry, such as legislation requiring that the dead be buried in English woollen shrouds in 1678 and again in 1700, proved ineffectual, as the desire to possess Indian cloth increased throughout the 18th century.

As the taste for the exotic and the new also extended to furniture, stout plain English oak was displaced by decorative lacquered chairs, tables and cabinets. However, as far as the Company business was concerned these were always eclipsed in importance by textiles and porcelain, which, being less bulky, were much more

102. The fashionable gentleman in this
Dutch print of *c.* 1690 wears a dressing
gown of Indian or Persian origin.

103. 'A Pagod Worshipp in ye Indies', from Stalker and Parker's *Treatise of Japanning and Varnishing* (1688). Recipes for the various types of japanning were published in this influential manual, as well as chinoiserie patterns that could be copied by amateurs and professionals.

profitable to transport. Unknown in the West before the European encounter with Asia, lacquer was immediately admired for its hardness, lustre, and decorative potential. An early example that reached London in 1619 was the ballot box used by the officials of the East India Company. Rather than from Japan, where lacquer had long been a speciality, the Company ships imported it from China with the name of 'Bantam ware' [27], after the Southeast Asian port from which it was obtained before becoming available on the Coromandel Coast of India (it went on being known as 'Japan' ware, and the technique as 'japanning'). It was formed by covering a wooden base with a mixture of brick dust, pig's blood and raw lacquer a few millimetres thick on a whitish foundation of clay, then layers of black or brown lacquer were applied, into which the design was cut until the white layers were revealed. The surface was further enriched by applying coloured lacquer or oil paint. The black-and-gold lacquer work mainly depicted landscapes, surrounded by decorative borders in the form of geometric designs, scrolls, and stylized flower heads.

Regularly imported into England, by the last quarter of the 17th century multi-leafed lacquer screens such as one at Erddig (probably a present from Yale) [100][19] and furniture made in European styles had become a familiar luxury in England. The effect of rich and splendid cabinets of red and black Chinese lacquer on gilt or silvered stands, such as were seen in the rooms of the Duchess of Portsmouth, was widely imitated by the 'japanning' technique [26], as instructed by John Stalker and George Parker in their *Treatise of Japanning and Varnishing* (1688), illustrated with many designs of Chinese gardens, pagodas, trees, plants, birds, beasts, and Oriental men and women [103]. Japanning was taught, like dancing, as a suitable accomplishment for well-born young ladies such as the eight-year-old Molly Verney, whose father Edmund paid a guinea for lessons and 40 shillings for materials to work on in 1682.[20]

The growing taste for luxury was further stimulated by imports of items from India inlaid with ivory and mother-of-pearl [20, 104, 108], or carved from ebony [105]. Designs were a compromise between the Eastern tradition and European taste. In 1700 the Joiners' Company stated in a petition that

> several Merchants and others trading to the East Indies and to several ports and places thereabouts have procured to be made in London of late years and sent over to the East Indies Patterns and Models of all sorts of Cabinet Goods and have yearly returned from thence such great Quantities of Cabinet Wares manufactured there after the English fashion by our models.[21]

Seat furniture, not in use in the East, was produced [22, 105], and copies were made of tables for eating and writing, and cabinets for use as portable writing desks or for display, to be mounted on stands [19–21]. Many such are recorded in the inventories of English country houses, where they passed down through successive generations. At Bedford House in London items dating from the life of the early 18th-century 2nd Duchess were listed in 1771: in Her Grace's dressing room were 'A dressing box of the rare old Japan, box neatly inlaid with ivory, and a stand for china of the rare old Japan', while the Red Drawing Room contained 'A cabinet of the old Japan with brass hinges and corner pieces on a carved and gilt frame' and 'A table of the old Japan on a partly gilt frame'.[22] The 1738 will of Celia Fiennes, who although not rich was an enthusiast for chinoiserie, lists bequests of 'Japan' and tortoiseshell cabinets, an ebony couch,

104. This fine bureau cabinet of teak inlaid with ivory, ebony and tortoiseshell, *c.* 1711–17, belonged to Governor Harrison [13]. While the piece with its double-domed cornice, arched doors, hinged fall front and fitted interior was designed for the European way of life, the ivory decoration of trailing flowers, trees in urns, birds and animals was a speciality of the craftsmen of Vizagapatam.

105. Indian furniture-makers used ebony, black and solid, for chairs such as these at Cotehele in Cornwall, with twist-turned frames and carved cresting at the back, made on the Coromandel Coast in the mid-17th century for the European market.

and a 'Japan' tea chest. Throughout the 18th century the taste was developed and continued, and while offering a more light-hearted alternative to the solid mahogany furniture and heavy damasks of the formal rooms, contributed to the profitability of the East India Company.

· · · · ·

At home in London, Yale surrounded himself with part of his own collection of Indian origin: in addition to furniture, textiles and jewelry there were hardstones, filigree vessels and gold boxes, paintings, sculpture, and weapons, so sought after by people of fashion. Each object must have recalled the picturesque world he had left behind, as Macaulay (himself in India from 1834 to 1838) wrote of Warren Hastings:

> the burning sun, the strange vegetation of the palm and the cocoa tree, the rice-field, the tank, the huge trees, older than the Mogul Empire, under which the village crowds assemble, the thatched roof of a peasant's hut, the rich tracery of the mosque where the imaum prays with face to Mecca, the drums and banners, and gaudy idols, the devotees swinging in the air, the graceful maiden, with pitcher on her head, descending the steps to the river-side, the black faces, the long beards, the yellow streaks of sect, the turbans and the flowing robes, the spears and the silver maces, the elephants with their canopies of state, the gorgeous palanquin of the prince, and the close litter of the noble lady . . . All India was present to the eye of his mind, from the halls where suitors laid gold and perfumes at feet of sovereigns to the wild moor where the gipsy camp was pitched, from the bazaars humming like bee-hives with the crowd of buyers and sellers, to the jungle where the lonely courier shakes his bunch of iron keys to scare away hyenas.[23]

These Indian artefacts, dispersed in his posthumous sales, were not only numerous but choice, and correspond with some that still survive. All over the house were modest dressing and powder boxes, but also an expensive writing box inlaid with mother-of-pearl, a speciality of Gujarat craftsmen [108].[24] Most of the items of hardstone – agate, cornelian and crystal – in the Yale collection were almost certainly of Indian origin, of a type much prized at the Mughal court [107]. During his travels in the mid-17th century, the French diamond merchant and great traveller Jean-Baptiste Tavernier [73] visited Cambay on the west coast 'where they cut those beautiful agates which come from India as cups, handles of knives, beads and other objects of workmanship'.[25] In this category come Yale's agate cups and salts, saucers, snuff boxes, numerous knives, forks, spoons, a small trunk, an 'Essense bottle enamelled and set with cornelians'[26] and a cornelian box and spoon, and silver-mounted crystal trunks, cups and boxes. The most expensive were 'a very fine ruby spoon the handle of gold' and several other gold objects: boxes, one set with stones, and an 'India gold snuff box enamelled at top'. His 'Toilet richly wrought with gold' and an 'India toilet' were probably versions of the grand silver and silver-gilt toilet services of the late 17th century.

It is difficult to establish whether Yale's collection of gold and silver filigree salvers, cups, boxes and trunks was made in India, for only the origin of '16 Curious Chinese Philligrew cups' is given.[27] However, a 'Ball of sweets garnished with gold philigrew' is most likely to be Indian, since it echoes 'An Indian Little Essense Bottle for Severall Sweetes' recorded in the schedule of the Countess of Devonshire's possessions in 1689 [cf. 107].[28] Described as of Indian craftsmanship were the following: a punch bowl and cover, three pieces of plate, a basin and stand, a large dish, beans (some silver-

mounted), gourd bottles, a waterpot with can (perhaps one of those carried by pilgrims [106]), 'an India brush' (perhaps a flywhisk), a drum,[29] a large wooden India teapot,[30] and an automaton 'India figure and bird moving by clockwork'.[31] An exotic group of large mother-of-pearl seashells and silver-mounted coconut bottles and cups is also likely to have come from the Indian subcontinent.

Besides precious stones and pearls from India, Yale owned jewelry made by native craftsmen, of the quality of the sapphire turban button bequeathed to the British Museum by Sir Hans Sloane [110]. A pair of gold bracelets set with rubies and sapphires, a collection of 121 gold beads set with rubies, a gold chain with talismanic snake stone in a gold box, and a splendid gold, emerald, ruby and diamond girdle were all of Indian origin. The jewels worn by rich Indian women and men, particularly the girdles [111, 112], impressed Europeans. In 1740 Mrs Benyon, married to the Governor of Madras, visited the wife of the person second in authority to the Great Mogul, seated in a pavilion at the end of a garden, and described her opulent attire to a friend:

106. A crescent-shaped pilgrim flask is carried on a pole over his shoulder by the attendant in the foreground, in a drawing of the procession of Rao Ratan of Bundi, c. 1625; it contained water for the journey to the shrine.

107. This scent bottle illustrates the Mughal technique of mounting rock crystal with a pattern of inlaid gold leaves and flowers encrusted with rubies and emeralds. It is still at Burghley House, where the Countess of Devonshire's possessions in 1689 included 'An Indian Little Essense Bottle for Severall Sweetes'.

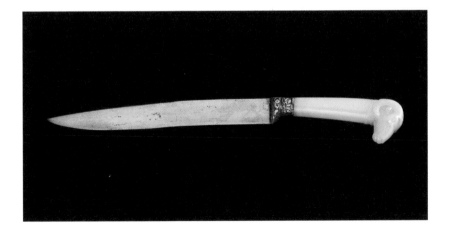

108. A travelling box decorated with mother-of-pearl set in black lac, from Gujarat, early 17th century. Yale owned several examples of this type of box with bevelled lid and pedestal foot. Used for storage, they were popular in Europe.

109. A knife with ferule overlaid with gold, and nephrite jade handle shaped by the Mughal or Deccani craftsman to form a naturalistic ram's head, transforming a functional object into a work of art.

110. Yale owned a pair of sapphire buttons;
this Mughal turban button, with a sapphire
held in a setting of gold and quartz with
emeralds and rubies, belonged to his friend
Sir Hans Sloane [53].

she had a fillet of diamonds round her head, edged with pearls of a large size, her earrings were as broad as my hand, made of diamonds and pearls, so that they almost covered each side of her face; she had a nose jewel that went through her left nostril; round her neck she had *twenty rows* of pearl, none less than a pea, but some *as large* as the *end of my little finger*, from her necklace hung a great number of rows of large pearl, which came down below her waist, and at the end of which hung an emerald *as large as my hand and as thick*; her coat was made of fine gold muslin, made close to her, and a short sleeve; a gold vail hung loosely over her head, and the rest went over her body, – all the front of it was trimmed with a row of *large pearls*. She had a girdle, or rather a large hoop, made of diamonds which went round her waist; it was above an inch broad; several strings of large pearls were tyed round her waist, and hung down almost to her knees, and great knots of pearls at ye end of them; ten rows of pearls round her wrists, and ten round her arms, a little above her elbows, and her fingers every one adorned with rings of all sorts and sizes; her feet and ancles were adorned much finer, *if possible*, than her hands and arms.[32]

Mrs Benyon went on the describe the luxury of the pavilion – the gold gauze curtains, the rich counterpane, the fine filigree candle-sticks, the containers of incense and sandalwood, and the gold filigree boxes of betel upon large scalloped silver trays. The presents for the Governor, Richard Benyon, were sent in a fine silver filigree box placed on the back of a fine horse adorned with gold and velvet trappings, and similar filigree objects, obtained by gift or purchase, must have been among those that Yale brought home to England.

Throughout his long years in Fort St George Yale had been involved in the purchasing, packing into bales, and shipping of at least fifty types of cloth (above, p. 29), it is reasonable to assume that some of the textiles in his sale were also of Indian origin.

111. The bejewelled young favourite of Sultan
Ali Adil Shah II of Bijapur, *c.* 1660, wears a
girdle to emphasize her slender waist.

112. Yale owned a jewelled girdle from India
which may have been similar to this Deccani
or Mughal girdle of gold set with diamonds,
rubies and emeralds.

113. Miniature from a *Ragamala* (garland of melody) album that was in the collection of Archbishop Laud before 1640, suggesting what some of Yale's 'small' Indian pictures might have looked like. This is Asavari Ragini, clad in a skirt of leaves like a tribal woman, charming serpents.

114. This 12th-century Pala sculpture of Vishnu was acquired by William Hedges, Governor of the East India Company's Bengal Station when Yale was in Madras. Given by him to the Ashmolean in Oxford in 1690, it was the first major Indian sculpture to enter a museum in the West.

Of the cloths listed, in addition to those that furnished his house in Queen Square (pp. 60–61), those intended for wear were a 'Fine needlework gown unmade' and a 'Fine Sattin Gown with Flowers of Gold not made up'. The many yards of fine muslin – striped, flowered, semi-transparent, dyed in various colours – reflect the uses to which it was put, which included men's cravats, women's 'wrought' (embroidered) aprons, veils and scarves, and the hand-kerchiefs used by snuff takers. The most sought-after muslins came from Dacca in Bengal (now Dhaka in Bangladesh), the less fine from Madras.[33]

Yale also owned paintings – several topographical views of Fort St George and also 'A large India Picture', whole-length portraits of 'three Indian Gentlemen', eight Indian kings, 'Indian birds painted on pieces of silk', 23 Indian pieces in glass frames, and another 23 Indian pictures 'small', which must indicate a taste for miniatures [113]. Indian paintings were on sale in London: Thomas Baker, in his play *The Fine Lady's Airs* (1709), introduces Mrs Furnish of St James's who had 'ordered lots of Fans and China and India Pictures', and Lady Rodomont, who, in response to an offer to show her some 'fine Indian pictures', replies 'I hate those shadows of men half finished' (she must have been thinking of portraits in the *nim qalam* technique, brush and ink with watercolour).

As for sculpture, in Yale's collection this was represented by figures in stone [114], and also figures in brass of women, a battle, a holy man at prayer, a lion and a bull. More numerous were the 'India figures carv'd in wood', probably representing the human and animal incarnations of the Hindu divinities, clothed, bejewelled and garlanded, carried in festival processions and perhaps represented too in painted woodcarvings decorating temple chariots [115].

115. Yale's numerous carved and painted wood figures may have come from chariots used in festival processions to the temple, drawn by horses, as in this model.

116. This Mughal *katar* or punch dagger of the 1630s, designed for hand-to-hand fighting, is powerfully functional and, with its gold handle enamelled with flowers and leaves and inlaid with rubies, luxurious.

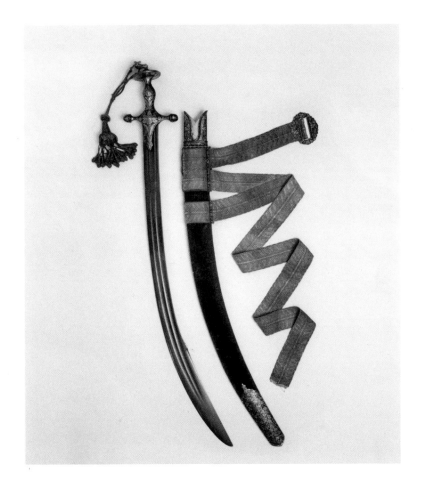

The numerous weapons in his collection included examples of the characteristic round shields and many daggers, some silver-mounted, including one described as a 'Curious India dagger head and case pure gold'. Most expensive of all were gold and jewelled hangers, that is swords with slightly curved blades [117], especially the 'Indian gold hanger set with diamonds and rubies' valued at £50.

117. The sword of the Mughal prince Dara Shikoh (Aurangzeb's brother), with its hilt overlaid with gold, curved blade of watered steel, and green velvet-covered scabbard with gold mounts, exemplifies the type of prestigious Indian swords with curved blades that Yale brought back. Constant warfare meant that there was a large supply.

3

YALE AND
THE ART WORLD
IN ENGLAND

In addition to living well, endowing his daughters, and support-
ing the activities of the Royal Society, his church, and charities
(including a small college in New Haven), Yale spent profusely on
buying European works of art and objects. In all, no fewer than ten
thousand items were dispersed in seven sales from December 1721
to April 1723. It is therefore surprising that his place in the history
of collecting and auctioneering in England should have been
neglected, especially as an analysis of his collection reveals him
as a man of his time, responding positively to new developments.
Thus his desire to acquire art on his return to London coincided
with the unprecedented expansion of the art world, which by the
middle years of the 18th century led to the establishment of the
city as the European centre for collecting.

Before the Civil War, with the exception of the Earl of Arundel,
English collectors were scarce, and they were overshadowed by
Charles I, whose great treasures were dispersed in the 1650s.
The tapestry-covered walls of the houses of grandees were hung
with few pictures, generally limited to family portraits; owing to
Puritan prejudice against religious works of art, there were virtually no examples of Italian Renaissance and Baroque painting and
sculpture. All this changed in the decades after the Restoration of
Charles II in 1660, when the English became Europe's greatest
art enthusiasts, creating a 'glorious heritage for posterity'. At first
collecting was the province of a few gentlemen connoisseurs, led
by the Duke of Shrewsbury and the Earls of Exeter, Manchester
and Carlisle. With the transformation of English intellectual life
symbolized by the activities of the Royal Society, a new generation emerged that was not confined to landed aristocrats but now
included 'middling people'.[1] To meet this growing desire to give an
impression of taste and erudition by owning and displaying pictures

and objects of *vertu*, professional and amateur dealers, auctioneers and artists converged on London. There was no problem with supply, since Italy had large stocks of surplus paintings accumulated over the centuries, and the art of the Northern schools crossed the Channel in quantity as a result of the slow economic decline of the Dutch Republic. In addition, immigrant artists, especially from Holland and the Southern Netherlands, were attracted to England, where they found employment copying Old Masters and producing portraits and popular genres, particularly landscapes, sporting subjects and decorative flower pictures. The success of Peter Lely and Godfrey Kneller, who were both knighted and maintained sumptuous houses, the high prices paid to Willem van de Velde father and son for their seapieces and to Simon Verelst for his sunflowers and tulips, encouraged native-born talent, led by Sir James Thornhill, who obtained important commissions.

The leading collectors from the aristocracy were the sharp-eyed 1st Duke of Marlborough, then buying for the gallery of Blenheim Palace near Oxford and Marlborough House in London, the 1st Duke of Chandos, the Earls of Pembroke, Derby and Halifax, Robert Harley, 1st Earl of Oxford, a great bibliophile, as was his son Edward, 2nd Earl of Oxford, and the 2nd Duke of Devonshire, brother-in-law of Yale's daughter Anne [18]. They set the pattern for English collecting by filling their country and town mansions with pictures from Italy and Holland, furniture from France, and finely bound editions of Italian, French and Latin authors. The young Wriothesley, 2nd Duke of Bedford (grandson-in-law of Sir Josiah Child), was typical. After inheriting no more than six paintings other than a group of family portraits, good, bad and indifferent, he began widening his artistic horizons by purchasing views of Rome during his Grand Tour. On his return he installed them above the doors of the great drawing room at Bedford House in London. From Italy he also acquired a set of four flower pieces by Niccolo 'Vanhoubracken' (van Houbraken) to hang in the dressing room of the Duchess. Another two flower pieces, guaranteed 'originals by Castile' (Peter Casteels of Antwerp), were supplied by the dealer Tristram Butler in Russell Street.[2] This buying came to an end with his early death in 1711, but had he lived he would certainly have assembled a large collection. There were so many others like him that during the reign of Queen Anne alone it was estimated by foreign artists that the nobility and gentry had secluded in their country halls as many pictures by renowned Italian masters as were found in the palaces and museums of Rome itself.[3]

There was also the knowledgeable collector Sir Andrew Fountaine [119, 136, 137], who knew Italy well and was adviser to the Earl of Pembroke. He was a friend of Jonathan Swift, who describes how they enjoyed London's refreshments and shops: 'I went to the City with him: we dined at the Chophouse with Will Pate, the learned woollen draper: then we sauntered at china-shops and book sellers, went to the tavern, drank two pints of white wine and never parted till ten.'[4] From 1717 the Whig statesman Sir Robert Walpole began spending the wealth he had acquired by speculation in insurance, in the Royal African Company, and in shares, by buying at auction a magnificent collection of pictures (later acquired by Catherine the Great and now in the Hermitage). Of the professional men who acquired paintings, works of art and manuscripts, the most successful, Sir Hans Sloane [53] and Dr Richard Mead, were both physicians, Henry Hoare was a banker, and Sir James Thornhill and Jonathan Richardson the Elder were artists.

Every week the newspapers published advertisements for sales of works from the European High Renaissance and Baroque, imported by dealers or from the estate of a deceased collector. The best-known picture dealers were Andrew Hay, a Mr Skelton, Mr Wicter, Mr Broom and Mr Castilles, who offered clients the chance of lengthy and proper examinations, and time to consider whether to buy or not. However, they were open to criticism. The old aristocracy and the new men with power and money competed to acquire works by the famous names of Italian and Netherlandish painting, leading the artist William Hogarth in 1737 to protest against

> picture jobbers from abroad who are always ready to raise a great cry in the Prints whenever they think their craft is in danger: and indeed it is in their interest to depreciate every English work as hurtful to their trade, of continually importing Ship Loads of Dead Christs, Holy Families, Madonnas and other dismal dark subjects neither entertaining nor ornamental: on which they scrawl terrible cramped names of some Italian masters and fix on us poor Englishmen the character of universal dupes.[5]

The concern over authenticity also arose from the widespread execution of copies, which could account for the vast number of pictures on the market, not only imported but also painted by foreign artists resident in this country. According to George Vertue in 1708 'one Turner a picture dealer comeing [over] to Antwerp' brought Peter Tillemans and his brother-in-law Peter Casteels to England, 'where he imployed them in their way. Tillemans made small pieces of his own Composition & copyed Bourgogione [i.e. Borgognone] for Battles, which he did many & of his own [designs] very well & landskips of other Masters coppyd extreamly well, at length gaining acquaintance amongst the [Virtuosi]'.[6] The wiles of cunning salesmen, and the fleecing of credulous clients, were the target of wits such as Alexander Pope and also Edward Young, who wrote:

... for what in oddness can be more sublime

Than Sloane, the foremost toyman of his time? ...

How his eyes languish! how his thoughts adore

That painted coat, which Joseph never wore!

He shows, on holidays, a sacred pin

That touch'd the ruff that touch'd Queen Bess's chin.[7]

As this lucrative market expanded, so did the practice of selling art at auction. One of the first such sales was held at the house of Sir Peter Lely in Covent Garden in 1680, arranged by Roger North. Afterwards he declared 'it was wonderful to see with what earnestness people attended this sale. One would have thought bread was exposed in a famine.' From this success sprang more auctions, usually held at the coffee houses around Covent Garden.

During the reigns of Queen Anne and George I and II coffee houses, as centres of social life, contributed greatly to the animation of the London scene, distinguishing it from all other cities [118]. In Queen Anne's reign almost five hundred coffee houses were listed, and every Londoner had his favourite where his friends could be sure to find him at certain hours.[8] The French observer Henri Misson thought them 'extremely convenient. You have all manner of news there: you have a good fire which you may sit by as long as you please: you have a dish of coffee, you meet your friends for the transaction of business and all for a penny if you don't care to spend more.'[9] They were first set up during the Commonwealth by a Turkey merchant who had acquired a taste for coffee in the Middle East. The convenience of being able to make appointments at any part of the town and being able to pass evenings socially at very small charge was so great that the fashion spread fast. Every man of the upper or middle class went daily to his coffee house

118. A London coffee house, 1695. In the
friendly atmosphere depicted Yale would
smoke his long clay pipe, drink, and talk. He
is also likely to have bought art at the auction
sales regularly held in his coffee house.

to learn the news and to discuss it. Every rank and profession, every shade of political and religious opinion, had its preferred establishment, for unlike clubs anyone could enter without being elected. Unusually, too, the coffee house brought different classes together: 'you will see blue ribbons and stars sitting familiarly with private gentlemen as if they had left their quality and degrees of distance at home'.[10]

Recognizing the power of advertising, the auctioneer J. Graham, at Three Chairs, Covent Garden Piazza, notified readers of *The Spectator* on 17 May 1711:

> I have travelled Europe to furnish out a Show for you, and have brought with me what has been admired in every Country through which I passed. You have declared in many Papers, that your greatest Delights are those of the Eye, which I do not doubt but I shall Gratifie with as Beautiful Objects as yours ever beheld. If Castles, Forests, Ruins, Fine Women and Graceful Men can please you, I dare promise you much Satisfaction, if you will appear at my Auction on Friday next.

Another auction of pictures, held by Mr Bressan at the Two Flower Pots by Somerset House in the Strand, was similarly advertised in *The Tatler* on 9 May 1710:

> A curious collection of Italian paintings by Giacomo and Leondro Bassan, Schiavone, Tintoret, Spagnolet, Nicola and Gaspar Poussin, Claude Lorain, Salvator Rosa, Fran. Bolognese, Mola, the Bourgognon, Luca Jordano, Bourdon and the Maltese, as also by Rubens and Van Dyck, the Velvet Breughel, Holbein, Brouwer, Berchem, Schalken, Teniers, lately brought from beyond the sea. Friday 18th inst catalogues to be had, views, today, tomorrow and Thursday before the sale at Somerset Garden.

OVERLEAF
119. William Hogarth shows the auctioneer Christopher Cock, who dispersed the Yale collection in 1721–23, displaying a painting for inspection by the eminent collector Sir Andrew Fountaine.

Jonathan Swift described how in January 1712/13 he 'sauntrd about this morning and went with Dr. Prat [Benjamin Pratt, Provost of Trinity College, Dublin] to a picture auction where I had like to be drawn to a picture that I was fond of, but it seems was good for nothing. Prat was there to buy some Pictures for Bishop Clogher who resolves to lay out ten pound to furnish his house with curious Peeces.' On 11 March Swift 'Layd out fourteen shillings', and next day he attended 'anothr Auction of Pictures today, and a great Auction it was'. He made Lord Masham 'lay out 40*ll* [£40], there were pictures sold of twice as much value a piece'. On 25 March Swift records another visit: 'Again with Pratt and there met the Duke of Beaufort.'[11] His reports prove that the London art market was expanding well beyond court circles and that the salerooms were open to a wide and enthusiastic public. Not all were impressed, and Edward Ward in *The London Spy* sounded a warning against the auctioneer's wiles: 'cozening and lying are the two most necessary talents to his profession . . . both put into practice as often as he has opportunity'.[12]

Whether it was by personal inclination to enjoy the pleasures of painting or by ambition to make his mark on London society, Elihu Yale was drawn into this world of collectors, dealers and artists. His example was followed by other nabobs; as Macaulay explained, 'having enjoyed great consideration in the East it was natural that they should not be disposed to sink into obscurity at home and as they had money and not birth or high connection it was natural that they should display a little obtrusively the single advantage they possessed.'[13] As the sales indicate, Yale had spent freely, acquiring more than seven thousand paintings, many attributed to famous old masters. Edward Harrison suggested that he might have been the dupe or 'bubble' of the dealers,[14] but how much Yale understood and how deep was his knowledge of art remain a mystery, for only a few of the pictures in his sales can be traced today. One can only hope that he did not resemble the nabob in a satire of 1785 by Henry Mackenzie[15] where Marjory Mushroom describes how the arrival of her newly enriched brother from India raised his simple country family to sudden but not always welcome affluence. In her opinion the great collection of pictures

> is the most plaguy of all his fineries. Would you believe it, Sir, he is obliged to be two or three hours every morning in the gallery with a little book in his hand, like a poor school boy getting by heart the names and the stories of all the men and women that are painted there that he may have his lesson pat for the company that are to walk and admire the paintings till dinner is served up.

What is not in doubt is the effect the sales of Yale's property had on the future of auctioneering. Joseph Haydn in his *Dictionary of Dates* of 1855 defined 'Auction' as 'a kind of sale known to the Romans, mentioned by Cicero, Livy and Petronius Arbiter', and went on to recognize the significance of the Yale auctions: 'The first in Britain was about 1700 by Elisha Yale, a Governor of Fort George, now Madras in the East Indies, who thus sold the goods he had brought home.' Outstanding advances in the dispersal of works of art were to be made as a result of the Yale sales by Christopher Cock [119]. An early patron of Hogarth, Cock is mentioned in 1717 by George Vertue: 'The picture of Mrs. Behn by Sr. Pe: Lelly at the Sale of Sir Geo. Hungerfords Pictures, sold at the Blew Posts in the Haymarkett on March 20.1716/7. Mr. Lovejoy & young Cock concernd.'[16]

Christopher Cock was making his mark, for a few years later he was engaged by the executors of Elihu Yale, and his success in disposing of some 10,000 articles in 3,600 lots vindicated their choice. He divided the lots from the London properties into seven sales between 14 December 1721 and 17 April 1723 – five lasting six days each, one of four days, and the seventh lasting three quarters of a day). For the first two sales, catalogues were available free from the place of sale (the house in Queen Square), and variously from Mr Osando's Chocolate House in St James's, the bookshop of G. and J. Inny in St Paul's Churchyard, Burton's or Button's Coffee House in Covent Garden, and Garraway's Coffee House at the Royal Exchange. Thereafter, as Cock's business flourished, catalogues could be obtained only from the house and from his own office 'near the Vine Tavern in Broad Street, near Golden Square' – the first professional premises belonging to a London auctioneer. Between 1723 and 1735 sale catalogues could be had from his Great Room in the Piazza, Covent Garden – the first of the leading London salerooms.[17] There, among other notable auctions, in 1733 Cock sold Sir Robert Cotton's nine Mantegnas, now at Hampton Court. In 1741–42 he sold the remarkable collection of the 2nd Earl of Oxford. The proposal put forward by his unsuccessful rival for that sale, Richard Ford, throws light on the many different aspects involved:

That the expense of putting the collection into proper Order for sale, taking and printing the catalogue, advertising in foreign and domestic papers, removing the collection, providing the place for sale, servants to attend and all other incidental charges shall be included in the rate of 5%. And all such single articles as shall sell at upwards of 40 or 50 pounds at a lower commission. The money to be received daily at the sale to be

The last SALE for this Season,
being the

Most Valuable Part

OF THE

COLLECTION

OF

ELIHU YALE, Esq;

(Late GOVERNOR of Fort St. George) Deceas'd.

CONSISTING

Of Jewels, (particularly that celebrated Diamond Ring, on which is cut the Arms of England and Scotland, formerly belonging to Mary Queen of Scots) fine Diamond and Pearl Necklaces, Gold repeating and Silver Watches, and Clocks with several Motions, Chas'd, Philligrew and Houshold Plate, with several Dozens of Silver Plates, and some Dishes; a large Collection of valuable Pictures and Limnings, among which is the Capital Picture of the Samaritan Woman, by the famous Vander Werf; a fine India Skreen standing upwards of ten Foot, with great Variety of extraordinary India Cabinets, and divers Sorts of useful Houshold Goods; Brass Cannons, Cerious Fire-Arms, Mathematical Instruments, fine Snuff Boxes, Swords and Canes, several Parcels of fine Silks, Linnens, Muslins, &c. With many valuable Curiosities in Gold, Silver, and Agate.

Which will be expos'd to View, at his late Dwelling-house in Queens Square near Ormond Street, Lambs Conduit, on Saturday the 2d of March, and every Day 'till the Time of Sale, which will begin on Thursday the 8th of March at Eleven a-Clock in the Forenoon precisely.

CATALOGUES to be had only at the Place of Sale, and at Mr. Cock's near the Vine Tavern in Broad Street near Golden Square, St. James's.

Conditions of Sale at usual.

(4)

10 A Japan Dressing-Table with Drawers, and two Indian Boxes on Frames — 0 10 0
11 Two small Indian Boxes, and a Corner-Cupboard, with a Walnut Tree Writing-Desk — 0 10 0
12 A Looking and Chimney Glass, in black Frames, six Glass Shafes, in lacker'd Frames, and two Glass China Rack — 1 0 0
13 Two Pictures, a Madona after Rubens, with an Ecce Homo.
14 Two ditto, a dead Christ, and a St. Magdalen.
15 Two ditto, a Madona, and a Visitation.
16 Two ditto, the Holy Family, and our Saviour bearing his Cross.
17 Two ditto, a Woman by Candlelight, and a Venus sleeping.
18 A Piece of Gause wrought with Gold — 1 0 0
19 Thirteen Yards of wide flower'd Thread-Sattin — 0 15 0
20 A fine blue and Gold Counterpane — 5 5 0
21 A Persian Quilt — 1 0 0
22 Eleven Yards of red and white Susee — 0 10 0
23 Nine Yards of fine Indian Dimitty at 3 s. per Yard.
24 Seven Yards and 3 qrs. of fine Muslin at 2 s.

Pictures.

25 Two Pictures, a Lady sitting for her Picture, and a Statuary's Shop, both on Copper.
26 Ditto, a Dutchman with his Family eating Mussels, and a Woman frying Pancakes.
27 Mr. Zeaman the Painter's Head, bigger than the Life.
28 Three Pictures, two Mens Heads, bigger than the Life, and a Lady's ditto.
29 King George at whole length in a Gold Frame.
30 Six Chinese Men, whole length.
31 Three Pictures, a still Life by Roestrate, two large Mastiff Dogs.
32 Sir John Wynn, half length, by Sir Godfrey Kneller.
33 Two, King William in Armour, and a Shepherdess, 3 qrs.
34 An old Philosopher's Head by Rimbrant.
35 Two, a Man with a Bag of Money, and a Siege after Wyke.
36 Two Views of Windsor Castle.
37 Two, a Sea-port on Copper, and a Piece of Flowers.
38 Ditto, a Dutch Merry-making, and Fruit, still Life.

China Ware, &c.

39 A large old China Beaker — 1 0 0
40 A blue and gold Jarr and Cover — 0 10 0
51 A

ABOVE RIGHT

121. A page from the catalogue of the first sale, in December 1721, listing furniture, Indian boxes, textiles, pictures and porcelain. Minimal descriptions are given of most lots, but here Christopher Cock gives details of some, including a self-portrait by Seeman (who painted Yale's portrait [1]), a portrait of Sir John Wynn by Kneller, and 'An old Philosopher's Head' by Rembrandt.

immediately taken by such persons as you shall please to appoint and the whole sale to be settled and the balance paid within 10 days after the sale. The disposition of the collection for sale and all the proceedings necessary thereto to be wholly submitted to your advice and approbation.[18]

It is also clear that the auctioneer was not able to deduct his fee from the money paid by the buyers, but had to wait until it came from the seller or his agent.

• • • • •

European paintings formed the largest group in Yale's collection, and exceed in number any sold at previous auctions in England. He might well have agreed with Joseph Addison, in *The Spectator* of 5 June 1711:

> When I have found the Weather set in to be very bad, I have taken a whole Day's Journey to see a Gallery that is furnished by the Hands of the Great Masters. By this means, when the Heavens are filled with Clouds, when the Earth swims in Rain, and all Nature wears a lowring Countenance, I withdraw my self from these uncomfortable Scenes into the Visionary Worlds of Art, where I meet with shining Landskips, gilded Triumphs, beautiful Faces, and all those other Objects that fill the Mind with gay Ideas and disperse that Gloominess which is apt to hang upon it in those dark disconsolate Seasons.

Moreover, in order to enjoy his pictures Yale did not have to move far from home. The house in Queen Square had high ceilings, and the framed paintings could be tightly hung together in several tiers on the walls, the larger canted forward like looking glasses, and perhaps displayed in the different rooms according to suitability of theme. There was not space to hang everything; works were stacked up on the floors, and others were stored near by in his stables and houses in Southampton Row [11]. Buying on this scale, although not indicative of connoisseurship, certainly shows enthusiasm, and the desire to possess and enjoy his paintings. Jonathan Richardson could have been thinking of the house in Queen Square when he wrote, 'Pictures are universally delightful and accordingly are made one part of our ornamental furniture.'[19]

Yale's collection was mainly of paintings, with only a few drawings and prints.[20] Since apart from miniatures no British school of painting had yet emerged, it was dominated by the works of foreigners. However, as Yale shared in full measure the traditional English interest in portraiture, he would presumably have supported the academy of painting and drawing from life established in 1711 by his neighbour in Great Queen Street, the celebrated Sir Godfrey Kneller, which was attended by Giovanni Antonio Pellegrini [99], Michael Dahl [123], Louis Laguerre, Jonathan Richardson the Elder [17], and James Thornhill.

As might be expected from such a dedicated upholder of the established order, English royalty is well represented. Demonstrating Yale's admiration for their sense of duty and respect for British freedoms are the many portraits of William III – his head, himself triumphant on horseback [122], in armour – and of his wife Mary II, which were probably copies made in the studio of Sir Godfrey Kneller. Queen Anne was similarly esteemed, judging from the number of portraits – heads, different lengths – depicting her [123], and also her husband, Prince George, and son, William, Duke of Gloucester, whose death in 1700 led to the succession of the King of Hanover as George I in 1714. Yale's support for King George is underscored by his portrait on horseback, and by a large family group. An interesting series depicts their predecessors on the throne of England: the Plantagenet Edward III, the Tudor Henry VIII (shown dancing with Anne Boleyn), and their daughter Queen Elizabeth I. The sequence is continued by the Stuart dynasty, which begins with Mary Queen of Scots, continues with her son James I and grandson Charles I, and ends with her great grandsons Charles II and James II. The portraits of the Duke of Monmouth, son of Charles II and of his mistress the Duchess of Portsmouth, were presumably painted by Lely. Outstanding contemporaries who were also depicted include the Lord Treasurer, the Earl of Godolphin, and his political ally, the Duke of Marlborough, whose four victories over the French armies in the War of the Spanish Succession were rewarded by fame, fortune, and the great Blenheim Palace in Oxfordshire. There was likewise a portrait of the Duke's strong-minded Duchess, Sarah, who shared and enjoyed his rise to almost royal status. Intriguingly, there were portraits of Marie de Médicis, Queen of Henri IV of France, their son Louis XIII, and their grandson Louis XIV, defeated so decisively by the Duke of Marlborough.

The few artists to whom portraits are attributed in the sale catalogues include Holbein, 'a man's head'; Cornelius Johnson (then working in London), '2 finely painted portraits of lady's'; Rembrandt, 'portraits of a General and of a philosopher and two heads'; Rubens, 'a head'; Kneller, 'Sir John Wynn'; and Seeman ('Mr. Zeaman the Painter's Head, bigger than the Life'. Most of the others, whether single heads or figures of children, old men, a nobleman in armour, a man writing, a cardinal resplendent in scarlet robes, a general, a young man in a ruff, or pairs of figures, such as that representing an old man with a boy, and another of a Dutch couple, are unattributed. Not all subjects are European:

122. At Fort St George, Governor Yale celebrated the accession of William III and Mary II in 1688, and back in London he expressed his loyalty, buying a portrait of the monarch on horseback as here, in armour, riding along the seashore over emblems of war. The King is watched by Neptune and greeted by Ceres and Flora; in the sky putti, Victory and Mercury hold up his helmet.

123. Queen Anne, depicted by Michael Dahl
wearing an ermine-lined cloak, her arm resting
on a plinth carved with oak leaves, symbolic of
the England she ruled.

there are a blackamoor, a Turk, sets of whole-length figures of Chinese noblemen (one of four, another of six, a third of twelve), and numerous Indians (p. 218). Since so little information is given, dating is difficult, except for a portrait of 'Fair Rosamund', mistress of Henry II, said to have been poisoned by his Queen, Eleanor, which might well have been inspired by the opera of that name written in 1707 by Joseph Addison.

The number of landscapes and townscapes in the collection reflects the abundant supply available, mainly from Holland, where artists were employed on a permanent basis by enterprising dealers such as Jacob de Witte.[21] By the 1690s so many English from the 'middling ranks' were buying pictures that a significant number of Dutch artists were resident in London.[22] This meant that most of the Yale landscapes are Dutch; only a few are by Italian artists, notably Salvator Rosa and Giovanni Benedetto Castiglione. The majority were oil on panel or canvas; some were on copper; and there were a few watercolours. Whether real or imaginary, these landscapes fitted well into domestic interiors, hung above mantelpieces or placed as overdoors. Besides several unidentified townscapes by Jan van der Heyden, there were views of London, one of them by 'John Wick' (Jan Wyck) depicting the Great Fire of 1666 [cf. 124]. At least eight of the earliest landscapes were neatly painted on copper by Jan Brueghel; a ninth is described as 'a Frost'. Picturesque views of mountains and waterfalls on larger canvases are attributed to Gerard van Edema[23] and Adriaen van Diest, both resident in London.

Most Dutch landscapes are enlivened with figures – a herdsman with cattle, a hunter with rabbits, a traveller on horseback talking to a man on foot – or with castles and other buildings. They were represented in the Yale collection by Jan Griffier, the younger Jan Wyck, and Nicolaes Berchem. Other landscapes with

OVERLEAF

124. As Yale had lived through the Great Fire of London, a dramatic depiction such as this would have brought back memories of the most terrifying experience of his youth. Yale's painting of the fire by Jan Wyck has not been traced, but the Dutch artist of this picture shows how the winds fanned the flames that destroyed the residential and business quarter between the Tower and the Temple.

figures and animals were attributed to Rubens, Cornelius van Poelenburgh, Roland Savery, and Philip Wouverman. Two landscapes by moonlight belonged to the genre of the nocturne, one of the most popular specialities of Dutch painting. A Classical note is struck by a landscape with sacrifice and ruins, 'finely painted'.

There were also views of beaches and of ports, one seen by moonlight, and studies of the sea, shown both calm and stormy. Seascapes were animated by ships both large and small and their crews. The artist to whom some of the Yale seapieces are attributed is Willem van de Velde the Younger, one of a family who specialized in this branch of Dutch painting, who was resident in England, installed at the Queen's House in Greenwich from 1672 [125].

The sale catalogues give no details of the subjects represented in the numerous history pieces, except for one by Rembrandt (who was not yet greatly regarded), nor is there any information about the battle scenes painted by the Fleming Adam Franz van der Meulen, by the Frenchman Jacques Courtois known as Borgognone, and by Thomas Wyck of Haarlem. Similarly, in architectural painting, except for interior and exterior views of Westminster Abbey, buildings are not identified but merely described as 'a piece of architecture' or 'a piece of perspective', a 'church interior', and 'a town on fire'.

Just as there were so many books on religion in his library, so there were numerous paintings in the collection depicting scenes and characters from the Old and New Testaments and from Church history. Beginning with the creation of Adam and Eve, the Biblical story continued with Noah and the Flood, Abraham offering up his son Isaac, Jacob's vision of the ladder reaching up to Heaven, his quarrel with Laban, and two events – the making of the brazen serpent and the drawing of water from the rock – that occurred as Moses led the Israelites out of Egypt. The young

125. *Calm: Dutch Ships Coming to Anchor*
by Willem van de Velde the Younger, *c.* 1665.

shepherd David, who became king, is shown with his wife Abigail and again on the roof of his palace watching Bathsheba, the beautiful wife of Uriah, as she bathed in the sunshine. In the next generation, their son Solomon, the third king of Israel, proves his wisdom in settling the dispute between two women both claiming to be the mother of a newborn baby. Another dispute, in which the virtuous Susanna was accused by the Elders, was resolved by the young prophet Daniel, who also warned the Assyrian king Belshazzar that he was about to lose his empire. Two other pictures depicted favourite subjects of Italian Renaissance and Baroque artists: the young Tobit with his father, and the heroine Judith dramatically displaying the head of the Assyrian general Holofernes.

The much larger series from the New Testament illustrated all the significant events in the Life of Christ and his Mother, the Virgin Mary, some of them in several versions. The sequence begins with the Annunciation, followed by the Visitation, the Nativity, the Adoration, the Flight into Egypt – shown by moonlight – the Massacre of the Innocents, John the Baptist preaching in the Wilderness, and his beheading. Christ's ministry is illustrated by the calling of Peter and Andrew, portraits of Luke and John, a large picture of the raising of Lazarus, the Feeding of the Five Thousand, the paying of the Tribute Money, and the expulsion of the money changers from the Temple. Christ's meeting with the Samaritan woman was shown in a painting on copper of 1717 by the immensely successful Adriaen van der Werff (bought at the sale by the Earl of Derby) [126].[24] The final phase, or Passion of Christ, was represented by the scene in the Garden of Gethsemane, followed by the Betrayal of Judas Iscariot, the Crowning with Thorns, the Carrying of the Cross, the Crucifixion, the Deposition, and the Entombment. While the Resurrection was depicted in a print only, events after it – the meeting with Mary Magdalen in the Garden, the doubting of Thomas, the Ascension – were recorded on canvas. In addition there was a large group of devotional images, mainly Italian, of the Virgin, Joseph, the Holy Family (one after Raphael), the head of John the Baptist, and the 'Ecce Homo'. Of these, two pictures – a Madonna and a Crucifixion – were attributed to Rubens and Van Dyck respectively, a 'small altar piece' to Albrecht Dürer, and a 'religious piece' to Holbein.

The history of the early Church was evoked by paintings of the conversion of Paul, Peter's deliverance from prison and martyrdom, and portraits of saints – Stephen, Augustine, Jerome, Antony, Christopher, George, Catherine and Cecilia – 'with flowers by Father Seaggers' (Daniel Seghers). As with his library of theological studies, Yale ranged widely – from a portrait of a pope to a 'Quaker's meeting on copper' and a hermit by Gerrit Dou [127]. Mention should also be made of the fine painting of the 'Institution of the Sacrament', sent from Rome as a gift to Wrexham Parish Church, and sadly no longer there.

Since Yale, like most men of his generation, knew Latin well, and through that language was familiar with Classical mythology and history, his paintings of the divinities of Mount Olympus must have given pleasure not only to his eye but also to his mind. Again, few artists are named, and almost none is Italian, but this category includes a Jupiter and Pomona described as 'a large picture by Rembrandt', a Venus by Albrecht Dürer, a Venus with Mars by a disciple of Rubens, and a Pan with Venus, 'a capital picture by Adriaen van der Werff'; Jupiter appears again in disguise as the seducer of Danae and of Leda.

126. One of the stars of the Yale collection:
Christ and the Woman of Samaria by Adriaen
van der Werff, 1717. This scene from the
Gospel of St John (4:4–30) was acquired
at the sale by the Earl of Derby.

127. Gerrit Dou, *A Hermit*, *c.* 1661. Dou
specialized in these small, highly finished
paintings of people and objects in candle-
lit rooms, much admired by Yale.

The many pictures of Venus – sleeping, as big as life, accompanied by nymphs, by a satyr, with Adonis, with her son Cupid, by candlelight, and receiving the Judgment of Paris – indicate a liking for nudes, as do Yale's paintings of Flora asleep and nymphs dressing. Other gods and goddesses include Bacchus – enjoying Bacchanalian revels, with Ariadne – and Diana, her brother Apollo with the Nine Muses, Ceres, the carrying off of her daughter Proserpine by Pluto, and the hero Hercules. Some illustrate stories from Ovid's *Metamorphoses*: Orpheus charming the beasts, Pyramus and Thisbe, Andromeda rescued by Perseus, Galatea, Narcissus, and the fall of Phaeton. There are two dramatic episodes from Homer's *Iliad*: the parting of Hector and Andromache and the burning of Troy, attributed to Hans Rottenhammer. Greek philosophy is represented by contrasting the laughing Democritus with the sad face of Heraclitus. As well as portraits of all twelve emperors and an empress, there are episodes from Roman history: a triumph, the Rape of the Sabines, the suicides of Lucretia and Cleopatra, and the filial piety of Pero giving the breast to her aged father Cimon in his prison cell.

Reflecting Dutch taste for the domestic and intimate are numerous examples of still-life paintings of flowers, food, vegetables, birds, fish and other animals. Yale owned finely painted flower pieces by the greatest Dutch specialists, Jan Davidsz. de Heem with his son Cornelis, and Willem and Simon van Aelst. The talents of this last were admired by Samuel Pepys, who on 11 April 1669 visited his studio and considered 'a little flower pot, the finest thing that ever, I think, I saw in my life, it is worth going 20 miles to see it'. A still life by 'Baptiste' could be by the French artist Jean-Baptiste Monnoyer; 'Mr. Bugdan', by whom Yale owned 'a festoon', must be Jacob Bogdani, a Hungarian, who lived near by in Great

Queen Street; Vertue says that he 'arriv'd to considerable talent in painting particularly fowles, birds of all kinds and nations in a pleasant agreable manner, with much beauty and softness & fruits and flowers in so much that he gain'd great applause & was much employd by people of Quality also Queen Anne in royal Palaces' [128].[25] Other depictions of flowers and fruit are attributed to Jan van Zoon and to Antonio Montingo, then working in London. De Heem combined some floral compositions with ripe fruit – grapes, oranges and strawberries – piled high in baskets on tables, or linked into festoons, displayed with silver cups and ewers, glass and fine linen. Although rarer, still lifes of fish, lobsters, dead game and fowl were well represented in the Yale collection. The list of birds is long: peacocks, parrots, ducks, hawks, pigeons, a cock and hen, a parrot (with a boy), and an owl 'painted from the life' by Jan van Zoon. 'A swan with other birds a capital picture by Wemyx' [129] was also bought by the Earl of Derby;[26] Jan Weenix, like Melchior de Hondecoeter, specialized in painting game pieces to hang in aristocratic castles and mansions.

Although one of the still lifes included a cat, animals were usually depicted out of doors. A painting by Roelant Savery contained a 'multitude of beasts and birds', but most showed just one or two, such as a ram's head, or a dog with a cat. Associated with the animal theme is a group of pictures of monkeys imitating humans – at play, smoking, sick, attended by the doctor – intended to amuse.

Genre was hugely popular in Dutch painting, and Yale liked it too, acquiring many scenes of everyday life [130]. Men are shown drinking, smoking, gambling, playing cards and eating eggs, and at work as doctors, surgeons, peddlers, soldiers, cobblers, farriers, park keepers, shepherds and chair-makers; there was a mountebank painted on copper by Rottenhammer. Boys eat mussels and play games.

128. Jacob Bogdani, *Still Life with Flowers in a Silver Urn, with a Monkey*, 1699. Yale owned a flower piece by Bogdani, who was also much liked by Queen Anne.

129. Jan Weenix, *Still Life with Swan and Game before a Country Estate*, c. 1685. Yale's house in Queen Square had been enriched by 'A swan with other birds a capital picture by Wemyx'.

Women read, sleep, nurse the sick, make sausages, sell fish during the day (on panels by Mieris) and fry fritters by candlelight, spin, cook and clean in the kitchen. Gentlemen are painted dressing and writing by candlelight; one elegant woman rides on horse-back, another goes to bed. Upper-class people hunt stags and shoot game. There is much music – ladies playing the harpsichord or a bass viol, boys fiddling and piping – merrymaking, feasting, and dancing. When these social scenes are crowded with good-humoured participants they are catalogued as 'conversations', with examples by Ostade, Egbert van Heemskerk (resident in London), and Teniers. In contrast, a note of warning is struck by 'an emblem-atical picture representing Gluttony and Poverty by Breughel', a robbery by 'old Wycke', and an execution, which illustrate the darker side of Dutch life and have a moral purpose.

Sets of prints of the 'Cartoons' were included in almost every Yale sale: these were after seven full-size designs by Raphael for tapes-tries commissioned by Leo X for the Sistine Chapel. The tapestries were woven, and the 'Raphael Cartoons' were eventually purchased in 1623 by the future Charles I; from 1699 they were displayed at Hampton Court (now in the Victoria & Albert Museum). Considered the greatest monument of Italian Renaissance art in England, they illustrate events from the Gospels and the Acts of the Apostles: Christ's charge to Peter, the Miraculous Draught of Fishes, the Death of Ananias, the Healing of the Lame Man, the Blinding of Elymas, the Sacrifice at Lystra, and St Paul preach-ing at Athens. In England the task of reproducing them in prints had been undertaken in 1707 and 1709 by Simon Gribelin, who produced a complete set, but in small dimensions. Mezzotints by Edward Cooper were on sale in 1710. Then in 1711 Queen Anne commissioned Nicolas Dorigny to produce larger prints at her

130. As an admirer of Gerrit Dou, Yale bought
a version of this atmospheric night scene of
a boy blowing on a firebrand to light a candle
by Dou's pupil Godfried Schalcken.

131. One of Nicolas Dorigny's engravings after
Raphael's Cartoons for tapestries in the Sistine
Chapel. This depicts the Apostle Paul blinding
the sorcerer Elymas before the Roman deputy,
who was converted (Acts 13:6–12).

expense to be given as official presents to the nobility and to foreign ministers.[27] The Queen lost interest when after three years he had completed only half the task, and had to bring assistants over from Paris, yet demanded a fee of £5,000. The Duke of Devonshire and other gentlemen proposed to finance the enterprise by subscription, a suggestion warmly supported by Richard Steele, who wrote in *The Spectator* of 19 November 1711 that it was impossible for a 'Man of Sense' to behold the Cartoons 'without being warmed with the noblest Sentiments that can be inspired by Love, Admiration, Compassion, Contempt of this world, and Expectation of a Better'. Yale subscribed, and owned several of the Dorigny versions, which were completed in 1719 [131]. He also owned another set in mezzotint, presumably those published by Edward Cooper, and versions in watercolour. He may have visited Dorigny's studio to see the work in progress, as Samuel Molyneux did in 1712: 'the prints are handed about everywhere . . . Mr. D showed us two plates which are finished and are indeed extraordinary. They are twice as large as the Mezzotints and do infinitely more justice to the Strength of Expression which is remarkable in Raphael's paintings.'[28]

Independent of the auctions was another important sale, that of the comprehensive collection of the poetic designs of Inigo Jones for architecture, masques and costumes evoking Jacobean court life: these were acquired direct from Yale's house by Lord Burlington,[29] and are still in the collection at Chatsworth [132].

Portraiture is the branch of painting most encouraged by the English, for, as *The Spectator* observed in December 1712, 'With respect to Face-Painting no Nation in the World delights so much in having their own, or Friends or Relations' Pictures', and in this category the miniature has the longest national tradition. The Yale catalogues, though giving few details, distinguish between the techniques of enamelled miniatures and of 'limnings' painted in watercolour and bodycolour on vellum, all designed to convey the likeness of an individual in little. Whereas enamel did not need protection, the watercolours were framed and kept under glass. In the Yale collection both techniques were used for portraits of Charles I and II, and also for Oliver Cromwell, represented by two enamels and by a limning framed in garnets. Miniatures of a lady and a gentleman, unfortunately neither identified, both in gold lockets, were described as by the greatest enameller of the time, Jean I Petitot [133]. The impressive number of contemporary works indicates that there was still a flourishing school of miniature painters to meet the continuing demand, although only one artist is mentioned. This was the enameller Charles Boit, who arrived from Sweden in 1687, was appointed court enamellist, and spent ten years in London making small copies of large-scale paintings as well as portraits *ad vivum*. The three examples of his work represented the 'Late Emperor of Germany' *c*. 1700, and two heads of gentlemen, one wearing armour [134]. There are several versions of each of the English monarchs, King William and Queen Mary, Queen Anne and her consort Prince George, and King George I, and single enamelled heads of Charles XI of Sweden and Louis XIV of France. Unidentified portraits depict men in armour, clergymen, and women, both young and old.

Although these portraits formed the major part of the collection of miniatures there was also a devotional group depicting Christ with the twelve Apostles, the Adoration, and St Francis. In another mood are landscapes, and scenes from history and mythology such as the death of Lucretia. Although designed primarily for the collector's cabinet, a few were intended for display as jewelry.

132. A drawing by Inigo Jones from Yale's collection, acquired by the Earl of Burlington. This is for one of the 'heav'n-born stars' in *The Lords' Masque* by Thomas Campion, performed at the Banqueting House in Whitehall in 1613. The published text explained: 'The ground of their attires was massy cloth of silver embossed with flames of embroidery; on their heads, they had crowns, flames made all of gold-plate enameled, and on the top a feather of silk, representing a cloud of smoke'.

133. The great Jean I Petitot was important enough to depict King Louis XIV of France, shown *c.* 1670 in armour with the blue sash of the Order of the St-Esprit. Yale had two miniatures by Petitot.

134. Yale owned a miniature by Charles Boit
of a gentleman wearing armour; this young
man was painted by him *c.* 1700.

Lockets were the most numerous, but there was a watch cover enamelled with the goddess Flora, and twelve 'very small heads' were set in rings. Jewelled frames surrounded some of the important portraits such as an enamelled head of King William that was bordered with diamonds, and a series of 'Limnings of all the kings of England from William the Conqueror to his present Majesty' were bound in a pocket book, 'the Covers of gold set with diamonds'. In addition there were miniature versions of the Raphael Cartoons, pastoral scenes, and a picture of Venus and Cupid, intended for insertion into the lids of the increasingly fashionable snuff boxes.

The Yale collection contained sculpture in various materials, which was no doubt displayed in Queen Square. Ivory from the tusks of elephants was an exotic material that he favoured. Soft, easy to carve, with a fine texture, it was used for various artistic purposes, but principally for display in collectors' cabinets during the 17th century. This development coincided with the expansion of maritime trade, especially round the east and west coasts of Africa, when more ivory was brought to Europe than ever before. Except for two groups of sixteen and eight figures respectively, described as Chinese, the rest of this part of the Yale collection could be European – Flemish, German or French – though not one piece is signed. Ivory handles are listed on swords, on knives and forks, on canes and staffs. The larger ivory cabinets were mounted on frames, the smaller were hidden in lacquer boxes. Devotional sculpture was represented by ivory crucifixes, one of the most characteristic themes of Baroque art, and Classical history by a Cleopatra. Of the portraits, only those of King Charles and Queen Anne are identified; the others are merely described as 'ivory bust of a man on a black pedestal', a 'busto on ivory', and 'a General in ivory'.

Also mentioned were twenty figures 'in ivory of different sorts' and carvings in high relief and low relief.

Besides these works in ivory and a set of amber chessmen, there were two lead figures of St George and a 'Shell curiously carv'd of the beheading of the Earl of Strafford' recording the event of 1641 that led to the Civil War, which are likely to have been English. Brass was well represented by images of women and of birds, by a Nativity 'finely chased', and by twenty-seven brass narrative scenes in low relief. Wood was carved and gilt in the Baroque taste, as Cupids, a sacrificial scene, and five figures with a layman. The most interesting group was '8 Scripture Stories in altra-relievo [*sic*] marble', perhaps Malines alabaster [135]. This was a popular art form, with images derived from prints of works by famous masters designed to be framed and used as private altarpieces.

Swept up as he was in the world of collecting, it was inevitable that Elihu Yale should acquire coins and medals, which he kept in cabinets and silver boxes. Thirteen silver medals of Queen Anne – Alexander Pope's 'Great Anna! Whom three realms obey' – demonstrated his support for the monarchy. His large collection of coins, which ranged from ancient Roman to those of his own time, included examples from the Tudors: Edward VI, Mary I and her Spanish husband Philip II, and Queen Elizabeth. The Commonwealth period was represented by crown pieces, known as 'breeches' because the arrangement of the two shields on the reverse side resembled a pair of trousers. These were estimated by Christopher Cock at their bullion value, by the ounce.

His collection could not compare in quality with that of his daughter Anne's brother-in-law, the 2nd Duke of Devonshire, but Elihu Yale shared the Duke's interest in hardstones engraved with portraits and scenes from Classical history and mythology.

His gems were mostly intaglios, that is with the image incised below the surface so that impressions could be taken for use as a seal [137]. Letter-writers liked to have their seals to hand, mounted in handles to place on the desk or to hang beside the watch [136]. Collectors preferred to set them in rings: they could be easily held up towards the light for viewing, and, if worn on the finger, were well placed when needed to seal a letter or document. Since they were nearly always very small, easily dropped and lost, for security reasons few were left unset. The hundreds of Yale cornelian, agate, and lapis lazuli seals were mounted in rings and in gold or silver handles, and a few groups were enclosed together in cases, as the 'ebony case with 18 intaglias finely cut upon several sorts of stones'.

The minimal descriptions in the sale catalogues of the lots, sold in groups of 12, 24, 35, 60, 100 and 120, give no indication of date, except for some described as antique, nor whether there were any signatures. A distinction is made between intaglios engraved with coats of arms and the antiques (with subjects from Classical art), and there are occasional specific references – to heads of Hellenistic and Roman rulers, Greek philosophers, 'a woman's head in fine onyx', a head cut in a large sapphire ring, histories, a bull, an onyx Vanity, and a 'Curious seal of a Venus and Cupid on an agate set in gold'.

Cameos, with the image carved in relief, are much rarer, but among them were onyx heads, one of a Roman emperor [138] and another of Cupid, and blackamoors, a favourite subject of Renaissance gem engraving. 'The Judgement of Paris curiously cut in agate by Routee'[30] depicts the choice of Venus as more beautiful than the goddesses Minerva and Juno. Two had Christian subjects: 'Our Saviour and the Virgin Mary's on an amethyst set in gold' and 'A Madonna in Agate cut in Altra Relievo set in gold enamelled'.

135. Malines alabaster relief of the
Entombment, from a late 16th-century
set representing episodes from the Bible,
suggesting the nature of the '8 Scripture
Stories in altra-relievo marble' in the
Yale collection.

136. Handle of the seal of Sir Andrew
Fountaine [119], of banded agate, gold,
enamel and diamonds, *c.* 1700. Like the
famous virtuoso, Yale possessed blackamoor
seal handles, then in fashion.

137. Sir Andrew Fountaine's seal, of banded
agate. His choice of Minerva, goddess of
wisdom, is an indication of his interest in
Classical art, which included gem engraving
as well as sculpture and coins.

267

268

138. The cameo representing a Roman
emperor in the Yale collection may have
looked like this onyx cameo of Augustus,
surrounded by a wreath of laurel.

There is little information about jewelled settings except for a man's head in coral flanked by two emeralds, and onyx heads set in two pairs of gold buttons and studs.

Among the curiosities stolen from Lady Fardingale, according to *The Tatler* in November 1710, there was a 'small amber box with apoplectic balsam', and Elihu Yale also owned objects made from amber, prized for its fragrance but also because it was thought to be efficacious against arthritis and diseases of the stomach. They were 'A fine Amber Draught box garnished with silver in a Case the Men of Amber', valued at £2, an 'Amber smelling bottle garnished with silver', and 'a head in high relief'. Tortoiseshell was used for snuff boxes, watch cases, and other objects such as porringers, silver-mounted trunks, bottles and cups [44, 46, 62]. Similarly horn, presumably from stag antlers, was carved into cups.

A miscellaneous group of curiosities included ostrich eggs (one carved, the other painted), two pieces of pinwork, one in a silver frame, and others representing two gentlemen's heads, and 'A very curious cabinet with Christal pillars the capitals of silver'. There were also two ship models, one in a walnut case, a moving fish, a small piece of waxwork, a waxwork baby that 'goes by clockwork', and a 'Curious piece of rockwork in glass frame'.

CONCLUSION

Of the works of art, jewels and objects from the Yale collection dispersed privately and in the sales held between 1721 and 1723, some of those that can be most securely associated with it – the diamond signet of Queen Henrietta Maria [86], the painting of Christ and the woman of Samaria by Adriaen van der Werff [126], and the drawings of Inigo Jones [132] – indicate the breadth of his taste and his eye for quality. Few, however, can be identified today, and as a consequence Yale's huge collection, assembled at considerable cost, has been virtually ignored by historians of the English virtuosi and of the art market in the early 18th century, and is rarely mentioned as a provenance. The auction catalogues with their minimal details are indeed (sadly) not of much value to the historian of art. To the biographer, however, they reveal Yale as a man who liked to live and dress well, surrounded by books and paintings, who maintained a lively interest in the arts, science and religion until the end of his momentous life.

What has made Elihu Yale famous is not his remarkable career in the East India Company, or his activities as an art collector: it is his philanthropy. As the Reverend Cotton Mather predicted (writing of him as of an Egyptian pharaoh), his pyramid, 'lofty and beautiful', is what became Yale University, which took root thanks to his benefactions at a time when the little Connecticut Collegiate School was struggling for its existence.

This great monument across the Atlantic in New Haven [140] contrasts with his modest burial place in his native Wales, in the churchyard of St Giles in Wrexham [139]. There his epitaph, composed by himself and inscribed on his chest tomb, succinctly sums up his career, hope of a future beyond the grave, and a warning to the living. It has been slightly altered over time, but was recorded in 1778 by Thomas Pennant in his *Tour in Wales*.

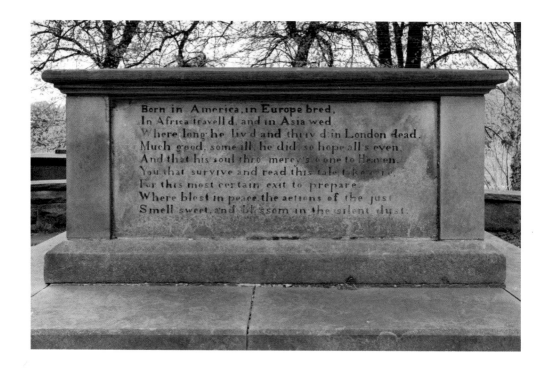

Born in America, in Europe bred,

In Afric travell'd, and in Asia wed,

Where long he liv'd, and thriv'd; at London dead.

Much good, some ill, he did; so hope all's even,

And that his soul, thro' mercy's gone to heaven.

You that survive, and read, take care

For this most certain exit to prepare:

For only the actions of the just

Smell sweet and blossom in the dust.

139. Yale wanted no more than this modest tomb in the graveyard of the parish church of St Giles in Wrexham, near his ancestral home of Plas Grono.

140. The great institution that he supported
when it was struggling to survive and that took
his name must also be regarded as a monument
to Yale. Virtually everything in this air view
belongs to Yale University, and there is more
beyond. Upper left is New Haven Green,
with its churches. To the right of it is the Old
Campus, and beyond that the Harkness Tower.

NOTES

PART I • CHAPTER 1
BOSTON TO FORT ST GEORGE
(Pages 9–39)

1 Edgar Samuel, *At the End of the Earth: Essays on the History of the Jews of England and Portugal* (London 2004), p. 251.
2 Bingham, *Yale*, p. 9.
3 Macaulay, review of *The Life of Robert Lord Clive* (1840), in *Essays*, pp. 503–4.
4 Macaulay, *History of England*, II, p. 304.
5 William Foster, *John Company* (London 1926), p. 10.
6 ibid., pp. 153–69.
7 ibid., pp. 171–84.
8 See Hickey, *Memoirs*, III, pp. 18–28, for a description of a hurricane at sea en route to India in 1769.
9 Foster, op. cit., pp. 70–81, and Spear, *The Nabobs*, pp. 10, 101.
10 Hickey, *Memoirs*, I, pp. 164–67, describes this method of transporting passengers and goods through the surf.
11 Trevelyan, *Life . . . of Lord Macaulay*, p. 263.
12 Quoted by Spear, *The Nabobs*, pp. 4–5.
13 ibid., p. 6.
14 ibid., pp. 8–9.
15 ibid., p. 10.
16 ibid., p.15.
17 ibid, p. 16.
18 ibid., p. 101.
19 ibid., pp. 11, 12, 14.
20 Trevelyan, *Life . . . of Lord Macaulay*, p. 323.
21 Bingham, *Yale*, pp. 36–37.
22 In return for exports from India, Europe exported both gold and the current silver coinage, 'pieces of eight', minted in Spain from South American bullion.
23 They included Sir Francis Bacon's *Elements of the Common Laws of England,* Richard Bolton's *Justice of the Peace,* John Rastall's *Abbreviation of English Law Books,* John Perkins's *Treaty of the Laws of England,* and Richard Brownlow and John Goldsborough's *Reports with Directions on How to Proceed in Many Intricate Actions.*
24 Bingham, *Yale*, p. 31.
25 ibid., chs vi–xi, cover Yale's rise to the position of acting governor and his mission to Porto Novo.
26 ibid., ch. xv.
27 ibid., chs xvi–xvii.
28 ibid., p. 273; and certainly the onset of his troubles coincides with the departure of Catherine.
29 ibid., ch. xxii.
30 ibid., p. 273.
31 ibid., p. 244.
32 This artillery is listed in the Yale sale catalogues.

PART I • CHAPTER 2
LONDON LIFE (Pages 41–55)

1 John Stow, *A Survey of the Cities of London and Westminster* (London 1720), quoted in Bingham, *Yale*, p. 310.
2 Molyneux, *London Letters*, Letter 6, pp. 128–30.
3 J. Kerr and I. C. Duncan, eds, *The Portledge Papers* (London 1928), p. 249.
4 Macaulay, review of *The Life of Robert Lord Clive* (1840), in *Essays*, p. 539.
5 Bingham, *Yale*, p. 306.
6 *Dictionary of National Biography* entry for Sir Charles Lodowick Cotterell.
7 Bingham, *Yale*, p. 303.
8 Macaulay, *History of England*, I, p. 19.
9 Trevelyan, *Life . . . of Lord Macaulay*, p. 228: 'for in their veins, too, flowed the blood of merchants, lawyers, country gentlemen and soldiers'.
10 *Gentleman's Magazine*, XXII (1732), II, p. 1015: 'younger brothers are generally condemned to shops, colleges and Inns of Court', and 'Younger sons are willing as cadets of the continental nobility were not to mingle in the army, law, trades, industry, commerce, keeping England supplied with high spirited young men not standing on their gentry.'
11 Roger North, *The Lives of the Rt. Hon. Francis North, Baron Guilford, . . . the Hon. Sir Dudley North . . . and the Hon. and Rev. Dr. John North* (London 1826), III, p. 231.
12 Marriage settlement between Anne Yale and Lord James Cavendish, 6 July 1708 (Centre for Buckinghamshire Studies, Aylesbury, D/CH/A/800), quoted by R. Ray, *Yale University Art Gallery Bulletin* (2012), p. 64, n. 30.

PART I • CHAPTER 3
AT HOME (Pages 57–81)

1 Brendan Lynch, who has most generously assisted me with this section, suggests that the 'Right India cabinet' could derive from 15th-century German flap-front types taken to Japan by the Jesuits and copied there in lacquer. Introduced to India, they were made in Sind and exported via Surat/Broach on the Gujarat coast. The phrase 'extraordinary cabinets' comes from the title page of the sale catalogue, 8 March 1722.

2 However, in spite of the auctioneer's description, we cannot always be sure of an Indian rather than Japanese or Chinese origin.
3 Amin Jaffer in *Encounters*, ch. 19.
4 Fiennes, *Journeys*, p. 387.
5 A. Bowett, *English Furniture 1660–1714* (Woodbridge 2002), p. 39.
6 ibid., p. 311.
7 Described by Celia Fiennes at Lord Orford's house, Chippenham Park in Cambridgeshire, in 1698. Fiennes, *Journeys*, p. 183.
8 Misson, *Mémoires*, pp. 313–14. The English stomach was for solid meat.
9 According to Anthony à Wood, *The Life and Times of Anthony Wood* (Oxford 1891–1900), III, p. 84, these bowls were named *c*. 1683 after 'a fantastical Scot called Monsieur Monteigh who at that time or a little before wore the bottom of his cloake or coate so notched'.
10 Bingham, *Yale*, p. 312.
11 Fiennes, *Journeys*, p. 153.
12 E. Standen, 'English Tapestries after the Indian Manner', *Metropolitan Museum of Art Journal*, 15 (New York 1981), pp. 119–42.

PART I • CHAPTER 4
GENTLEMAN OF FASHION
(Pages 83–97)

1 The wind or air gun was an unusually early example. The carbine was a short light gun of intermediate size favoured by horsemen, which hung by the side on a belt passed over the shoulder under the right arm.
2 Lady Mary Wortley Montagu, *Complete Letters*, II, p. 24.

3 *Lettres de Madame, duchesse d'Orleans, née Princesse Palatine*, ed. Olivier Amiel (Paris 1981), letter of 4 February 1714.
4 Alastair Leslie, *Three Hundred Years of Tobacco Stoppers* (2012), describes various types used to press down the tobacco into the bowl of the pipe.
5 The box was made by Paul de Lamerie. Victoria & Albert Museum, London, Gilbert Coll., loan 665-2008.

PART I • CHAPTER 5
THE PLEASURES OF MUSIC, BOOKS, AND SCIENCE
(Pages 99–131)

1 Baruch Spinoza, *The Correspondence of Spinoza*, transl. and ed. A. Wolf (London 1928), p. 100.
2 Macaulay, *History of England*, I, p. 199.
3 Lady Mary Wortley Montagu in a letter to a Mr X in 1716 mentions 'a small piece of Loadstone that held up an Anchor of Steel too heavy for me to lift'. *Complete Letters*, I, p. 279.
4 Spear, *The Nabobs*, p. 101, and n. 33, quoting from Captain Symson, *New Voyage to the East Indies*.
5 Diana Scarisbrick, 'Documents for the History of Collecting 3: the Earl of Carlisle's Gems', *Burlington Magazine*, CXXII, no. 1007, Feb. 1987, p. 90.
6 Quoted in his book *Watches*, p. 58, by David Thompson of the British Museum, to whom I am grateful for imparting his knowledge and drawing my attention to examples similar to those owned by Elihu Yale.
7 Misson, *Mémoires*, p. 239.
8 Either Ahasuerus Fromanteel or his son John.

9 Established English makers preferred this type of watch, which functioned with the greatest accuracy.
10 A pair-cased watch is defined by David Thompson in *Watches* as 'a watch in which the movement is housed in an inner case which itself is then contained in a second outer case'. A repeater is a watch designed in the 1680s to indicate the hours and the quarters, or even the hours, quarters and minutes, by striking a bell or gongs or by tapping a block inside the watch case. So that the sound of the bell could be heard, the cases were often decorated with openwork ornament.
11 Probably due to the difficulty of fitting the alarm in the new layout after the adoption of minute hands.
12 Presumably Princess Caroline, the highly intelligent wife of the future George II.
13 *The Spectator*, 4 Dec. 1711: 'there is a new invention by D. Delander of a spring, which is very neatly fix'd to the outside, and will prevent the cases being lost or stolen. This spring is to be fix'd to all manner of watch cases.' Quoted in Thompson, *Watches*, p. 68.
14 John Gay, *Trivia, or the Art of Walking the Streets of London* (London 1716), bk III, ll. 345–50.

PART I • CHAPTER 6
PHILANTHROPIST (Pages 133–145)

1 Bingham, *Yale*, p. 219.
2 ibid., p. 188.
3 ibid., p. 324.
4 D. Wing and M. Johnson, 'The Books given by Elihu Yale in 1718', *Yale University Library Gazette*, Oct. 1938, pp. 46–67. Also J. Walker Straus,

Book Collections of Five Colonial College Libraries: A Subject Analysis, unpublished PhD thesis, University of Illinois, 1960, pp. 150–52.

5 Exceptionally, one gun is attributed to Brooks, the only maker identified in the collection. Another curiosity was a 'fowling piece left handed', very rare and extremely difficult for use by a right-handed sportsman. The twelve steel crossbows listed in the sale might have been used for shooting smaller birds. Also for sporting use were Yale's hangers – swords with a slightly curved blade and ornate handle.

6 Trevelyan, *English Social History*, p. 370.

PART II • CHAPTER 1
A FORTUNE FROM JEWELS
(Pages 149–185)

1 Bingham, *Yale*, p. 305.
2 Yogev, *Diamonds and Coral*, p. 143. This study is an indispensable guide to the subject.
3 Samuel, 'Gems from the Orient: the activities of Sir John Chardin (1643–1713) as a diamond importer and East India merchant', *Proceedings of the Huguenot Society*, XXVII, 3 (2000), pp. 351–68.
4 Bingham, *Yale*, p. 184.
5 Letter from Thomas Pitt to Sir Stephen Evans, 7 Jan. 1703/4, quoted by Colonel Yule, *The History of the Pitt Diamond*, Hakluyt Society (1888), p. 4.
6 Tavernier, *Travels*, II, p. 68.
7 ibid., p. 61.
8 George Fox, history of the firm Rundell, Bridge and Rundell. Manuscript in the Baker Library, Harvard University Library; typescript copy in the National Art Library, Victoria & Albert Museum, London, 276, E 3.

9 Yogev, *Diamonds and Coral*, p. 69.
10 Bingham, *Yale*, p. 237, and E. Samuel, 'Manuel Levy Duarte (1631–1714), an Amsterdam merchant jeweller and his trade with London', *Jewish Historical Society of England Transactions*, XXVII (1982), p. 22.
11 Yogev, *Diamonds and Coral*, p. 140.
12 ibid., p. 139, n. 65.
13 Samuel, 'Gems from the Orient' (above, n. 3), p. 364, explaining the collapse of the diamond market.
14 *The Wentworth Papers 1705–1739*, ed. J. J. Cartwright (London 1883), p. 164.
15 J. E. B. Mayor, ed., *Cambridge Under Queen Anne* (Cambridge 1911), p. 406.
16 J. A. Rouquet, *The Present State of the Arts in England* (London 1755), p. 90.
17 Lady Mary Wortley Montagu, *Complete Letters*, II, pp. 19, 42–43.
18 Samuel, 'Manuel Levy Duarte' (above, n. 10), p. 23.
19 R. E. Raspe, *A Descriptive Catalogue of ... Engraved Gems ... cast ... by J. Tassie* (London 1791), p. vi.
20 Diana Scarisbrick, *Jewellery in Britain 1066–1837* (Norwich 1994), p. 166.
21 Lorenz Natter, *Traité de la méthode antique de graver en pierres fines, comparée avec la méthode moderne* (London 1754), p. xv.

PART II • CHAPTER 2
A NEW WESTERN TASTE
FOR THE EAST (Pages 187–221)

1 Evelyn, *Diary*, pp. 460–61.
2 ibid, p. 756.
3 Thomson, *Russells*, pp. 327–28.
4 *Mercure Galant*, 1678.
5 Macaulay, *History of England*, I, p. 683.
6 ibid.

7 Lady Mary Wortley Montagu, *Complete Letters*, III, p. 97.
8 Irwin and Brett, *Chintz*, p. 2, n. 6.
9 *Encounters*, p. 268.
10 Fiennes, *Journeys*, p. 308.
11 ibid., p. 387.
12 Thomson, *Russells*, p. 97.
13 Irwin and Brett, *Chintz*, p. 6.
14 Beverly Lemire, *Fashion's Favourite: the Cotton Trade and the Consumer in Britain 1660–1800* (Oxford 1991), p. 59, quoted in *Encounters*, p. 270. Lemire surveys the relationship between Indian cotton imports and fashions in Britain. I owe this reference and other valuable information relating to textiles to Dr Sonia Ashmore of the Research Department, Victoria & Albert Museum, London.
15 Irwin and Brett, *Chintz*, p. 30.
16 Trevelyan, *England Under Queen Anne*, I, p. 98.
17 *Encounters*, p. 270.
18 Macaulay, *History of England*, II, p. 308.
19 Merlin Waterson, historian of Erddig, has suggested that the lacquer screen there was a gift from Yale to his neighbour. Joshua Edisbury had sent a present of 'four roundletts of sandpatch ale' to Yale at Fort St George. Elihu's letter of thanks dated 1682 is still preserved with the Erddig papers in the Clwyd Record Office, and there he promised to send in return a japanned screen. Waterson also suggested that the silk of the curtains of the state bed at Erddig was brought back by Yale.
20 F. P. and M. Verney, *Memoirs of the Verney Family during the Seventeenth Century* (London 1907), II, p. 312.

21 Quoted by Amin Jaffer in *Encounters*, p. 258. These models were known as 'musters'.
22 Thomson, *Russells*, pp. 342–44.
23 Macaulay, review of *Memoirs of the Life of Warren Hastings* (1841), in *Essays*, p. 652.
24 Simon Digby, 'The mother of pearl overlaid furniture of Gujarat: an Indian handicraft of the 16th and 17th centuries', in Robert Skelton, ed., *Facets of Indian Art* (London 1986), pp. 213–22.
25 Tavernier, *Travels*, I, p. 68.
26 There was a long tradition of enamelling in North India at Jaipur.
27 Some of the best filigree came from Orissa (Cuttack). For 17th-century filigree caskets see the collection of the National Museum, Lisbon.
28 A. Somers Cocks, *The Countess' Gems*, exh. of 16th- and 17th-century jewels and artefacts as recorded in the Schedule of 1690 from the collection of Burghley House, Stamford, held at the house (1985), pp. 26–28.
29 Hawker drums, elephant drums and military kettle drums are depicted in miniatures. See for instance musicians celebrating New Year at the court of Shah Jahan, in the Royal Collection *Padshahnama*, folio 70v.
30 Brendan Lynch suggests this might have been Tibetan, for tea with yak milk.
31 Sir Thomas Roe recorded court fascination with clocks, automatons, etc. W. Foster, ed., *Journal of Sir Thomas Roe* (Hakluyt Society, 1899).
32 *The Autobiography and Correspondence of Mary Granville, Mrs. Delany*, ed. Lady Llanover (London 1861), II, pp. 169–73. (She spells the name 'Binyon'.)

33 Flowered muslin was usually embroidered in white on white, though at this period the best quality designs – *jamdani* – were figured on the loom, and were accordingly very expensive. I am grateful to Dr Sonia Ashmore of the Victoria & Albert Museum for making this point.

PART II • CHAPTER 3
YALE AND THE ART WORLD
IN ENGLAND (Pages 223–269)

1 Iain Pears in *The Discovery of Painting* surveys this development in detail, quoting from excellent sources.
2 Thomson, *Russells*, pp. 135–40.
3 Trevelyan, *English Social History*, p. 305.
4 Swift, *Journal*, I , p. 43.
5 *St James's Evening Post*, June 1737.
6 Vertue, Note Book III, p. 14.
7 Edward Young, *The Love of Fame or the Universal Passion*, Satire 4, 1730.
8 Trevelyan, *English Social History*, p. 324.
9 Misson, *Mémoires*, p. 180.
10 Trevelyan, *English Social History*, p. 324.
11 Swift, *Journal*, II, pp. 593, 636, 645.
12 Edward (Ned) Ward, *The London Spy* (London 1703, Folio Society 1955), p. 212.
13 Macaulay, review of *The Life of Robert Lord Clive* (1840), in *Essays*, p. 539.
14 Bingham, *Yale*, p. 306.
15 Henry Mackenzie, 'Letters of Marjory Mushroom', in *The Lounger*, Edinburgh, 1785.
16 Vertue, Note Book I, p. 43.
17 Peter Ash, 'The Great Yale Auction', *Estates Gazette* (26 Aug. 1961), pp. 507–8.

18 Quoted in Pears, *The Discovery of Painting*, p. 64.
19 Jonathan Richardson, *An Essay on the Theory of Painting* (London 1725), p. 1.
20 The drawings (including watercolours) and prints are merely listed as 'landskips' and 'heads', e.g. '40 heads history in watercolours some framed, 12 ditto with landskips, framed View of St George'.
21 Denys Sutton, 'Augustan Virtuosi', *Apollo*, Nov. 1981, p. 324, quotes Vertue, Note Book III, p. 14. Also W. Martin, *Burlington Magazine*, XI (1907–8), p. 363, discusses Dutch and Flemish forgeries. In 1706, Jan van Bredael spent four years in Antwerp making copies after 'Velvet' Brueghel, Wouverman and others for Jacob de Witte, who was active from 1689 to 1702.
22 C. Gibson-Wood, 'Picture Consumption in London at the End of the 17th century', *Art Bulletin*, 84, no. 3 (Sept. 2002), pp. 491–500.
23 His works were in various English collections: Vertue, Note Book I, p. 93, Mr Edema 'waterfalls'; p. 131, 'Many pieces are done by him for this nobleman [the Earl of Radnor] some of his best'; II, p. 37, '2 waterfalls painted by Edema' at Chatsworth.
24 Russell, 'The Derby Collection 1721–35', p. 169: bought for £327 12s., it hung in Lady Derby's dressing room.
25 Vertue, Note Book I, p. 127.
26 Russell (above, n. 24); bought for £23 2s.
27 Chia-Chuan Hsieh, 'Publishing the Raphael Cartoons and the Rise of Art Historical Consciousness in England 1707–1764', *Historical*

Journal, vol. 52, 4 (Dec. 2009), pp. 899–920.
28 Molyneux, *London Letters,* Letter 3, p. 68.
29 Vertue, Note Book I, p. 110.
30 Probably John Roettier, medallist and gem engraver employed at the London Mint, who, according to Evelyn (Diary, 20 July 1678), 'emulates even the ancients in both metal and stone'.

BIBLIOGRAPHY

Hiram Bingham, *Elihu Yale* (New York 1939)
Encounters: the Meeting of Asia and Europe 1500–1800, exh. cat., ed. Anna Jackson and Amin Jaffer, Victoria & Albert Museum (London 2004)
John Evelyn, *Diary,* ed. E. S. de Beer (London 1959)
Celia Fiennes, *The Journeys of Celia Fiennes,* intro. John Hillaby (London 1983)
William Hickey, *Memoirs of William Hickey,* ed. Alfred Spencer, vol. I (8th edn, London n.d.), and vol. III (2nd edn, London n.d.)
John Irwin and Katharine B. Brett, *The Origins of Chintz* (London 1970)
T. B. Macaulay, *Essays* (London 1889)
—— *History of England* (London 1889)
Henri Misson, *Mémoires et observations faites par un voyageur en Angleterre* (The Hague 1698)
Samuel Molyneux, *The London Letters of Samuel Molyneux 1712–13,* intro. and ed. Paul Holden and Ann Saunders (London Topographical Society, 2011)

Lady Mary Wortley Montagu, *The Complete Letters of Lady Mary Wortley Montagu,* ed. R. Halsband (Oxford 1966–67)
Iain Pears, *The Discovery of Painting: The Growth of Interest in the Arts in England 1680–1768* (New Haven and London 1988)
Francis Russell, 'The Derby Collection 1721–35', *Walpole Society,* 1987, 53 (1989)
T. G. P. Spear, *The Nabobs* (London 1932)
Jonathan Swift, *Journal to Stella,* ed. Harold Williams (Oxford 1948)
Jean-Baptiste Tavernier, *Travels,* ed. V. Ball (n.p. 1889)
David Thompson, *Watches* (London 2008)
Gladys Scott Thomson, *The Russells in Bloomsbury 1669–1771* (London 1940)
G. M. Trevelyan, *England Under Queen Anne* (London 1930–34)
—— *English Social History* (London 1946)
G. O. Trevelyan, *Life and Letters of Lord Macaulay* (London 1889)
George Vertue, *The Note Books of George Vertue relating to Artists and Collections in England* (Oxford: Walpole Society), I, vol. XVIII (1930); II, vol. XX (1932); III, vol. XXII (1934)
Gedalia Yogev, *Diamonds and Coral: Anglo-Dutch Jews and Eighteenth Century Trade* (Leicester 1978)

LIST OF ILLUSTRATIONS

Dimensions are given in centimetres, followed by inches in parentheses

BL = The British Library, London
V&A = Victoria & Albert Museum, London

INDEX

ACKNOWLEDGEMENTS

This biography, which covers so many different aspects of the life of Elihu Yale, could not have been written without the generous contributions of friends and colleagues, all experts in their fields. Diana Scarisbrick acknowledges with deep gratitude the advice received from Robert Skelton, Susan Stronge (Victoria & Albert Museum), Brendan Lynch, and Roselyne Hurel (Musée Carnavalet, Paris), which helped her follow Elihu Yale's career in the East India Company and assess the significance of his acquisitions of Indian art and objects. She is also indebted to Sonia Ashmore (Victoria & Albert Museum) for her advice on the Yale collection of textiles, to Angus Patterson (Victoria & Albert Museum) and David Edge (Wallace Collection) for arms and armour, to Chris Nobbs (National Trust) for musical instruments, to Jolyon Hudson for the Yale library, to Dr Louise Devoy (British Museum) for scientific instruments, to David Thomson (British Museum) for clocks and watches, and to Richard Stephens and Jeremy Warren (Wallace Collection) for guiding her through the early 18th-century London art world. Benjamin Zucker thanks Jock Reynolds, Jay Ague, Derek E. K. Briggs, Edgar Samuel, Jack Ogden, Robert Lloyd George, Judith Ann Schiff, Nicolas Norton, Jonathan Norton, Francis Norton, Romita Ray, Basie Bales Gitlin, Jay Gitlin, Robert W. Gray, Susan Stronge, and Derek J. Content for the enlightening and enjoyable conversations that have brought him closer to the mind of Elihu Yale and shed light on his career in India, his activities as a diamond dealer, and his involvement in the cultural and intellectual life of London. Both authors have benefited greatly from the professional skills of Julian Honer, editorial director of Thames & Hudson, the imagination and tenacity of Jo Walton, our picture researcher, the taste and ingenuity of the designer, Alex Wright, and, most of all, the exemplary dedication and enthusiasm of our editor, Emily Lane.